life is
more beautiful
than paradise

Life is More Beautiful than paradise

A Jihadist's own story

Khaled al-Berry

Translated by
Humphrey Davies

The American University in Cairo Press
Cairo   New York

First published in 2009 by
The American University in Cairo Press
113 Sharia Kasr el Aini, Cairo, Egypt
420 Fifth Avenue, New York 10018
www.aucpress.com

Dar el Kutub No. 4109/09
ISBN 978 977 416 294 7

Dar el Kutub Cataloging-in-Publication Data

al-Berry, Khaled
     Life Is More Beautiful than Paradise: A Jihadist's Own Story / Khaled al-Berry.—
  Cairo: The American University in Cairo Press, 2009
       p.   cm.
       ISBN 978 977 416 294 7
       1. Arabic fiction   I. Davies, Humphrey. (trans.)   Title
       892.73

1 2 3 4 5 6 7 8   14 13 12 11 10 09

Designed by MacGuru Ltd.
Printed in Egypt

Contents

To Jood

Preface

What does being a member of an Islamic group mean? To put the question differently, how does a member of a jihadist group see himself, his family, his childhood friends, the society around him, and the world?

Is the stereotype of jihadists true? Alternatively, is a jihadist an ordinary person who makes a certain choice, not out of hatred but out of love?

I never thought for a moment that my own experience with the Jamaʿa Islamiya, or The Islamic Group, could be of interest to anyone. Yet I was wrong. Three people were interested in it: a Lebanese student of sociology, Liliane Daoud, her professor at the Lebanese University, Dr. Waddah Sharara, and his friend, Mohamad Abi Samra, editor of the cultural supplement of Lebanon's *an-Nahar* newspaper. They encouraged me to write this book. I would therefore like to express my gratitude for the interest they showed and for all they have done to ensure that this book saw the light.

The first edition of this book appeared in July 2001. At that point, the work consisted of nothing more than articles brought together as part of a series of "Testimonies" published by *an-Nahar*. These articles, or stories, were written with a journalistic brevity calculated to whet the reader's appetite and provide quick reading, no more.

Two months after the appearance of the first edition came the attacks on New York and Washington, and the world started snapping up as fast as it could any books that discussed Islamist groups. The work was therefore issued in French, Italian, Spanish, and Dutch translations. As time passed, that first bout of enthusiasm quite naturally dissipated, and a more objective approach to the book as literature rather than journalism took its place. This manifested itself when a UK publishing house indicated its interest in publishing the work and showed it to a professional editor, who wrote a report setting out a number of points that needed to be expanded on because they were unclear, as well as a proposed division into what he deemed logical sections. I found this report extremely useful and as a result revoked the promise I had made myself never to revisit the work, even by reading it. I took advantage of a free period following publication of my novel *Nigatif* (Negative) and made what modifications I could. Two further specialized editors in two publishing houses then read it and came to the same conclusion – that further changes were needed, including the removal of some repeated material. More importantly, it became clear that the repetitions were the result of the organization of the narrative by topic rather than chronologically, something that made disjunctions unavoidable.

The last time I made changes to the book, I did so out of love for the work, not in response to professional demands. This third time, I was depressed following the theft of my laptop, which contained the sole draft of a novel on which I had worked hard. I found, however, that dividing my work time between refashioning *Life Is More Beautiful than Paradise* and rewriting the stolen novel reduced the pressure on me, and the two processes fed into one another. The writing of the novel brought greater fluency to the biography and the biography inspired an interest in detail that was applicable to the novel.

Finally, I cannot conceal my feelings of pain at disclosing information about individuals whose joys and sorrows I shared over a long period and at the thought that any of them might get the false impression that I intend to harm them in any way by so doing. It would also be painful to me should the readers of this book think that these men who were my 'brothers' in the Jama'a were in any way evil people.

Such pains, however, are not sufficient to make me apologize, and will never stop me from speaking.

The English translation that you are now holding reflects a fourth reworking (published in Arabic in 2009 as the second Arabic edition). I have introduced a small number of changes to it in order to correct minor factual errors and misprints in the Arabic editions or improve comprehensibility for non-Muslim readers. I will be giving no secrets away if I say that this is the first version of this book that I have been satisfied with.

1

Paradise

It was just a poke in my shoulder. Sure, he followed it up by pushing his face up close to mine, but the beginning was just a poke in the shoulder. It made my brain stop working. What could I do against him? Should I poke him back? If I did so, he'd beat me ignominiously for sure. Should I walk away? That would be an unforgivable sign of weakness and my friends would never let me live it down.

It was broad daylight, and there was nowhere to hide from the ordeal, or the scrutiny. My other friends were standing round but no one intervened to hold him back – which would, at least, have been a way for me to get out of it with dignity. None of them said a word as they stood there, waiting to see what I'd do. He stuck his nose against mine and kept up his threats. I raised one hand but he struck it down hard. He wanted me to stand as stiff as a solider at attention while he spoke to me. I raised my other hand and he hit that hard too. I had to do something. I ran away and picked up a rock and came back toward him, looking mad and threatening. He didn't move. He just looked me steadily in the eye; all I could think of as an excuse was to pretend that my knees had given way and to fall to the ground at some distance from him. It was obvious, laughable, pitiful cowardice, no doubt, but I had no other option when faced by this youth who was older than us. Unlike the rest of my childhood friends, he'd appeared only about three years ago. He'd gone out into the big world before us, and was ahead of us in his experience of sex and of teenage life; he smoked and drank alcohol and told us about the major fights he got into along with his friends, or his gang, against anyone who got in their way in that world of which we knew nothing. He and his friends were capable of tracking down their rivals to a café or hashish den, giving them a good thrashing, and pulling the place down over their heads. Or so he said. It wasn't to be expected of me that that I'd stand up to the youth, even if the price was that I'd have to avoid going out to play with my friends so that I wouldn't have to put up with his mockery of me. I stayed at home for several days, for this hardened veteran of the streets beat up on the guard of our building, who was two years my senior but much shorter than I. This guard used to say that those whom God had created dwarves built up stronger muscles to make up for what they'd been denied by way of height. The well-known Egyptian proverb, "I'll thrash you and I'll thrash anyone who dares to defend you," had come true.

I was almost fourteen. My voice had begun to change, becoming deeper. I had outgrown the embrace of childhood that permitted weakness and indulged crying. It was impossible, for me as much as for my friends who'd witnessed the scene, to forget about the knee pain that I'd faked. My sense of myself and of my relationship to the world could no longer ignore the society in which I lived. I was now like that society. It too was a society with a rough voice, and a mustache. It too was a society that had no time for weak knees. That same year, it became apparent that I wasn't the only one to reach that conclusion.

That year, the events known in Egypt as the Central Security Incidents took place. We were in school that day and were surprised to hear the administration asking us to return directly to our homes. The area in front of the school gate filled with the cars of hundreds of families waiting for their children. My family wasn't waiting for me, however. The Opel '68 that was all that had been left of the estate of my grandfather, who had died when I was two, had been sold the year before, and I was forced to go home on foot, totally unaware of what was going on. On my journey back to the house, I was accompanied by a youth whom I knew through a distant family connection. He told me that what had happened might be a repetition of what had taken place in Asyut five years before, when, two days after the killing of Egypt's president, Anwar Sadat, the Jama'a Islamiya had attacked and tried to take over the city's police headquarters. Those were events I'd lived through myself, when I was nine, and they had ruined the Feast of the Sacrifice for me, for which I criticized the Jama'a bitterly.

When I got home, however, I discovered that what had occurred this time was simply a mutiny by police recruits throughout Egypt, and that the sole point of resemblance between it and the earlier events was that anger had been translated into violence, shooting, and the burning of cars, nothing more. The Central Security Incidents were not the doing of an organization that aimed to overthrow the regime or possessed ideological goals. It was anger, pure and simple. What was important was that this event opened the way for me to a closer acquaintance with the youth who kept me company on my way home, because we met again a few months later and he reminded me of what I'd said about the Jama'a Islamiya when I'd thought it was behind the violent incidents. I repeated my opinion to him, in a few words that I'd memorized from my father: "Abdel Nasser understood them and imprisoned them. If he'd let them alone, they'd have killed him the way they did Sadat." We had some friends with us. Some agreed and some didn't.

The gathering broke up and I was left alone with the boy I'd gone home with. He asked me if I knew any members of the Jama'a Islamiya and I said no, even though a few years before I had known one – one whose name, in fact, had a very special place in the history of the Jama'a Islamiya. My friend condemned me for expressing such harsh opinions when I didn't know them and gave a different account of them. He was dazzled by their acts, by their 'heroism,' and by the 'glory' they'd earned by their commitment to their religion, for *glory belongs unto God, and unto His Messenger and the believers* as it says in the Qur'an (8:63). Then he promised to make me a gift of a bicycle chain that could be used to hit people during fights. He himself had been taught how to use it by the Jama'a and possessed a number of such chains that had been made into weapons by disconnecting one of the links of the chain to make it straight, not circular, and by wrapping one of its ends in adhesive plastic.

A few years before, I'd got to know Antar. He worked in a small restaurant that sold beans and falafel close to our house, and during the vacations I'd see him every morning. He'd joke with me and my sister and ask me about the soccer league match results. "Watch!" he used to say, challengingly, and set about rapidly chopping tomatoes, or squeezing out from the ring formed by his thumb and index finger a ball of bean paste ready to drop into the oil; if he noticed me in the midst of the throng, he'd serve me quickly so that I didn't have to wait. One night in 1979, I was doing homework with one of the neighbor boys in his apartment upstairs, and the sound of demonstrations against the Camp David Accords came to us from the outside, though we couldn't see anything. The grownups talked of the Accords as treason; this was the indisputable consensus in both my neighbors' households and my own, and it was not to be questioned. What the grownups said was not open to debate: they knew things we didn't and they listened to the news and could recall events we had neither lived through nor could find in the history books. That wasn't all, though, for the following day we learned that Antar had been killed in the demonstrations. So it definitely was treason. The day Sadat was killed was one of the happiest of my childhood, along with the day when Ahli football club – fielding only youth players and substitutes – beat Zamalek's first team by three to two, and the day when my parents bought me a bicycle as a reward for getting a score of 97.5 percent in the Elementary Certificate exam. I asked my uncle on my mother's side, who was a recent graduate of the Police College, if the police really had gone into a mosque without taking off their shoes during these demonstrations, and he smiled and didn't answer. I asked him about Antar too. He was talking to my mother and his sister, and to him my queries were just "kid's talk." I was very fond of that uncle, but I didn't like the police, because they were "unjust people."

Antar was in the Jama'a Islamiya and against the regime, but "Uncle" Ahmad, the newspaper seller, was different. Ever since we were little, waking to his cries of "Akhbar! Ahram! Gumhuriya!" had been one of the characteristic markers of a vacation. He would cut a bit off a cigarette packet to form a ring, which he'd wrap around the paper before throwing it up onto our balcony. If I woke up before he came, I'd wait for his arrival and go out onto the balcony and throw him a clothespin to use in place of the paper ring, especially during cigarette shortages. Sometimes I'd go down to the street and ask him if I could throw the paper up onto the balcony. Either way, doing so guaranteed that I'd be the first to read the sports page, and to find out the name of the Arabic film that would be on TV in the afternoon. I'd also discover whether an episode of *The Six Million Dollar Man* would be on the *We Have Chosen for You* program that evening. If it was a Thursday or a Sunday, I'd make sure he didn't forget to deliver the *Mickey Mouse* and *Samir* comics with the paper. If I was lucky, I'd run into Uncle Ahmad on his donkey cart, either very early in the morning or after he'd finished his rounds, and be given a ride. Once this cart, or rather the donkey that pulled it, didn't stop when a police car was crossing an intersection in front of it, as cars did when they had the bad luck to happen on a passing police car. The officer got out of the car and, violating every rule of Upper Egyptian manners, slapped the man, who was old enough to be his father, on the face. From then on I was too embarrassed to joke around with Uncle Ahmad. I felt that I ought to make myself look sad whenever I saw him, out of respect for his feelings.

I spent the night dreaming of the bicycle chain, just the way I used to dream that I was Bruce Lee, after seeing a movie of his, or Muhammad Ali Clay, after seeing a movie about him. The next day went by, and the day after, and the boy with the chain didn't come back. In such small towns, however, people's fates walk hand in hand. We owned two buildings in Asyut that stood opposite one another and rented out the basements to students. In one of these lived two bearded students whom I'd met at the soccer pitch. Once, I'd gone down to say hello to them and found one of them trying to remove the nail of his abscessed big toe with a switch blade, during which operation he went on talking to me and laughing as though it were nothing. His capacity to withstand pain was amazing. I mentioned him to my friend who'd gone home with me that day and whom I shall refer to from now on as 'the Chain Boy,' and he confirmed what I'd said, describing the student I was talking about as a "first-rate brother." He followed this with tales of his bravery, which he employed in the defense of religion and the disciplining of wrongdoers, and which, as a result, was unsullied by pride or arrogance – and which was, indeed, part of his kindly and modest nature. Such were the things that distinguished the observant, courageous brother from the lowlife tough who used force to lord it over God's creatures.

It is difficult for a person to comprehend why he loves what he loves, or even to know what it is he loves. Till then, I'd been a boy of weak physique, outstanding at his studies. I differed from the friends I mixed with on the street in that I went to a private school, that of the Soeurs Franciscaines, which meant, as far as I was concerned, that I had to wear a shirt and pants while they wore government-school smocks, and that I could challenge them to spell the name of my school, which they couldn't. My general interests were reading and the cinema, which I started going to regularly on my own every week from the age of ten. I was a 'patriotic' adolescent who, as was natural for his age, knew little of the Great, or Small, Powers, or the balances and calculations of politics. I parroted such common expressions of the day as "the One Arab People" and "the Arabs are a people known for their glory, pride, and generosity," and blah blah blah-de-blah. I listened often to the speeches of Abdel Nasser and the patriotic songs of Abd el-Halim Hafez and I hated Sadat, 'Camp David,' and Israel, without bothering myself with the details. At the start of the previous school year, new maps had turned up in our classroom showing 'Israel' where 'Palestine' had once been. We protested to the school administration and refused to hang up the maps, and in the end the administration gave in and took them away. The same year, I fell behind while marching to the classroom in the morning lineup to the rhythmic strains of the school band, and an angry teacher stopped me and slapped my face. That day I decided this was no place for me and that the noblest thing I could do in life would be to leave school and join a group training fedayeen for operations against Israel. I didn't know any such groups, assuming that they in fact existed, but the idea obsessed me for two whole days and I spent much time teaching my younger brother, who was six, to repeat the sentence "We must fight Israel to the last man."

Naturally, I forgot all about it when I stopped being angry.

My small family, consisting of a father, a mother, a sister four years older than me and a brother eight years younger, lived in a quiet neighborhood of Asyut called Qulta Company. Traditionally, this neighborhood had been the well-off part of that southern city. Other parts of town had now, however, overtaken it in terms of property prices and, like any other older neighborhood, the nature of its residents was changing as time passed and social paralysis set in. Despite this, its streets remained busy because of its proximity to the university, whose presence when in session caused the number of Asyut's inhabitants to more or less double. For older buildings, such as the two that belonged to us, renting out to students brought in a reasonable income that compensated for the meager yield from the apartments. In the basements of both our buildings, and on the roof of one of them, in cheap, badly ventilated, poorly appointed rooms, lived students from the countryside who were unable to pay the rent of a furnished apartment. From time to time, the students from the basement apartments would come to my father to complain that the drains had flooded their rooms and soaked their books and bedding, while the students from the roof would come during the rare rains to complain that their rooms had been turned into pools of water by the rain coming in through the wooden ceilings. It was from students such as these, and those in the other buildings near the university, that the majority of the younger members of the Jama'a Islamiya was drawn.

Some of these students shared my love of soccer. Soccer lovers among the Jama'a Islamiya were careful to include others in this team sport that was impossible to play properly when there were only one or two, or even three, players in a corner of a big pitch. I took to playing regularly with them in spite of the inconvenient time that they had chosen – after the dawn prayer on Fridays. I knew many of them by name and from time to time would run into them when they went down our street on leaving the university and would go with them to the mosque to pray. From chatting with them, I came to learn much about their personal lives. Brother Ashraf, the handsome one, had once loved to gamble and used to walk around the Imbaba quarter of Cairo with a pack of cards poking out of his shirt pocket as an invitation to others who might want to play; now, however, he was one the Jama'a's most promising preachers. Ala', an engineering student, had been unable to enter university for the past year and had abandoned his hopes of a degree because the security forces were after him. Tal'at's parents were big-time merchants in Minya, but he had sacrificed their wealth and his life of ease with them to engage in Islamist activity. And there was Mahmud, whose father was supposed to enter the prosecutor general's office but who died in a motorcycle accident the very day he was appointed.

One month after I had got to know these "virtuous people" and become a regular attendant at prayer with them, I went to Cairo, where my uncles on my mother's side lived and which, for me, bore no resemblance to the city in which I lived. Before leaving for Cairo, I informed one of the brothers that I was going there because it was the only place where you could get training in kung fu. He advised me not to go. Up to that point, the Jama'a had been associated above all else in my mind with the image of the strong Muslim, of the fedayeen band made up of strong people who prayed and fasted. I asked the same brother why he didn't want me to go to Cairo to get trained when he himself was very good at kung fu and had been trained in it. He told me that if I went to Cairo I would lose my commitment to the brothers and that, "To be a committed brother and not good at kung fu is much better than to be good at kung fu and not a committed brother." All the same, I wanted to learn kung fu, and also to work during the summer vacation so that I could be more independent. I went to Cairo.

I didn't get kung-fu training there because I was too lazy to look for a place where I could get it. There was the ESCO Club, close to Shubra el-Mazallat where the uncle I was staying with lived but I was ... just plain lazy. I didn't have any real motivation. Soccer aside, I was always like that with sports. I'd get training in a sport for two weeks, then abandon it. That was how it had been with swimming, table tennis, handball, and even weightlifting.

As far as the other side of things – work – was concerned, my uncle took me to a cheap café and introduced me to the owner, telling him that I wanted to work for him, "even though his father owns two apartment buildings in Asyut." Of course, this wasn't exactly true; it would have been more accurate to say that my father and his fifteen brothers owned those two buildings. All the same, I liked his way of putting it because I felt it would be useful in determining the kind of work the café owner chose for me. In fact, at the time, I loved to hear others refer to my family as a family of distinction, which it was, though only by certain standards. My paternal grandfather was a rich countryman. My father had often told me of the telephone directory that bore his father's name at a time, in the fifties, when few people owned telephones, and of the electricity generator that provided light for his father's houses and those of the rest of my family at a time when the villages of Egypt were without electricity. My father was himself only the second person in the village to obtain a university degree. All this was true. However, when my grandfather died in 1974, the not-insignificant amount of money that he left was quickly spent and all that remained to us were some buildings and land that couldn't be sold because of the shame attached to the sale of property – that, and the memories related to us by the generation that had witnessed and had had the pleasure of enjoying these things. We too committed these stories to memory as they were told to us and believed in them faithfully. Only two years previously, my best friend had been a boy named Ahmad, whose father was dean of the College of Medicine at the University of Asyut. Ahmad lived in the classy housing set aside for the university professors, where the buildings were surrounded by greenery and playgrounds, and where there was a swimming pool. I used to go every week and play with him in this faculty housing area, and I continued doing so for three months or more. One Thursday evening in summer when I was there, a youth some years older than me came over and told me that he'd seen me often at 'the Housing' and didn't want to see me there again. Ahmad wasn't far away, and he must have known what the youth was going to tell me, but he didn't interfere or do anything to stop him. Indeed, he didn't even ask me, as I left the place in tears, why I was leaving and not waiting so that we could play together as we usually did. From that day until I joined the Jama'a Islamiya, I didn't exchange with him more than such passing words as were necessitated by our being in the same class. The sole acknowledgment of distinction I received was from the nuns at my elementary school when they collected contributions every Thursday and would ask me to pay more. I never enjoyed any of the special treatment that some of my colleagues, especially those who were sons of police officers, university teachers, or doctors, received. On one occasion, I obtained the highest marks in Arabic Language in the monthly schoolwide exam, and the teacher reduced my score because it wasn't right that I should get better marks than the student who was both best in the class (in everything except Arabic Language) and the son of a professor at the university.

The restaurant owner looked at me for a moment and then called over one of his workers and asked him to show me what to do. The worker waited until a customer got up from his table, then he picked up a cloth and wiped the table, removing the dishes and saying, "This is what I want you to do." He looked at me when he'd completed his demonstration and said, "There's a customer about to finish over there. Show me what you're going to do." I informed him that I had to make a quick trip to the nearby mosque to get my copy of the Qur'an, which I'd left behind there by mistake when I was performing the ablutions before prayer. I went to the mosque and didn't find my Qur'an, but of course I didn't go back to the restaurant. I contented myself throughout the entire month that I spent in Cairo with sitting at home and listening to music. I even stopped going to Friday prayers, preferring to stand on the balcony watching the girl in the apartment opposite dancing to the song "On the Way" by Muhammad Fu'ad.

When I returned to Asyut, I was met by the same brother who had warned me against going to Cairo and he asked me why I wasn't going to the mosque. I stammered out some general excuses. He looked me in the eye and said, "Tell me honestly, old friend, do you still pray?" I couldn't answer. Up to that moment, I'd never told a lie, this being one of the strict moral principles that my mother had taken great care to instill in me. She had had sole responsibility for raising me during my early years, up to the age of six, because my father had gone to Yemen to teach on secondment. The same principles had been further instilled in me at my school, which was run by nuns.

Following this incident, I began to attend prayers more regularly and only postponed them if there was a soccer match on
television. I began going more often to the mosque for the com-
munal prayer that is "twenty-seven times better than individual
prayer" (Hadith). At the mosque, I got to know Sheikh Tareq, one
of the kindest and most sincere people I have ever known. He
agreed with us that he would organize daily lessons at the mosque
at which we would learn the principles of Islamic jurisprudence,
the Sunna, and the life story of the Prophet. The lessons were concerned exclusively with general principles and made no reference
to the specific thinking of the Jama'a Islamiya. Sheikh Tareq had
a small restaurant where he sold the round sides of bread filled
with hashed spiced meat and onions known as hawawshi. There
we'd eat sandwiches that he made especially for us and spend the
evenings in long conversations from which we learned even more
than we did from the formal lessons. Sheikh Tareq had so much
love and affection for others that his every word seemed meaning-
ful, and he made you love him and love every word he uttered
and every idea he believed in. He bore a scar on his chest from an
operation he'd had on his heart. When I first met him he was in his
mid-twenties. I don't know when he'd had the operation, though
I believe it may have been performed while he was in prison for
three years following the events of 1981. What I do know is that he
continued to practice his religion faithfully and didn't use his condition as a way of claiming that he was incapable of undertaking
the activities in support of the Islamist cause that his commitment
entailed. Similarly, though his restaurant was well known and
the security forces could have arrested him easily and cut off his
source of livelihood, he never used this as an excuse to abandon
his activities. He was an exemplary man – bold and unflinching
despite the vulnerability of his livelihood and health. And on top
of that, he was from the same town as the eminent Islamist thinker
Sayyid Qutb.

Sometimes I would fail to appear at Sheikh Tareq's lessons
because of a movie or soccer match that was being shown on
television at a time that conflicted with one of the prayers, most
often the late afternoon prayer. Sheikh Tareq seemed to have

understood this, so he asked me to prepare a presentation on the Islamist position with regard to music to deliver to my colleagues in the study circle. I told Sheikh Tareq quite frankly that I would find this unpleasant to do as I loved music so much and couldn't imagine myself stopping listening to it. "Who said you should stop listening to it?" asked Sheikh Tareq. "Just research the sayings of the Prophet and the verses of the Qur'an that talk about music, see how the scholars of religion have interpreted them, and set it all out for us." Then he gave me, to help me in my task, a copy of *Talbis Iblis* (The Insinuations of Iblis), a book that deals with the stratagems that Iblis, the Devil, resorts to, to seduce humankind. The word Iblis sounded pleasant to my ear; I couldn't describe it as beautiful, because it described the Devil, but it was musical, poetic. It had been engraved on my mind by the incredible delivery of one of the preachers at Friday prayers when he declaimed the Salafist verses that go:

Iblis, the world, my self, and desire –
What road can I take, when all are mine enemy?

I shut myself up in my room to listen to the songs of Mayyada el-Hennawi while I leafed through the book, noting the various scholars' opinions on a piece of paper. I emerged with a summary that said that music was forbidden by religion and that anyone who listened to a female singer would find that "on the Day of Resurrection, *anuk* – which means molten lead – would be poured into his ears" (Hadith). I also discovered that the most that Islam permitted in the way of music was the beating of the *duff*, or large tambourine. I wrote this down and took it with me to the mosque. There, I sat in the circle of students, holding the paper with trembling hands, and read it to my friends. After the lesson, Sheikh Tareq congratulated me on the quality of what I'd written and praised the effort I'd made. He put me on notice, however, that now that I had become aware of the issue, I bore a greater responsibility, and that God's reckoning with me would be tougher if I persisted in disobedience while well aware of His judgment on the issue.

As I wiped clean all my music tapes (except for the one with Abd el-Halim Hafez singing patriotic songs), I gave no thought whatsoever to singing itself, or to its importance to me. As far as I was concerned, listening to music was just an act, a simple act, the abandonment of which would permit me to prove to myself my sincerity and determination to obey the divine prohibition. This was the first real lesson that I learned with the Jama'a Islamiya – what was Halal and what was Haram, what was permitted and what was forbidden. What was forbidden was everything God had prohibited, and what was permitted was everything else. This was the view adopted by those who supported the idea that religion should be 'lenient.' At the same time, if something new was compared to something old that some text prohibited, then the new thing was forbidden by analogy, even if no clear text prohibiting it existed. This simple step of mine was followed by another that I could never have imagined. The next time I failed to attend afternoon prayer it was to watch a soap that I liked. This time, Sheikh Tareq himself undertook to explain the position of religious law with regard to those who looked on a woman whose body was not adequately covered, whether in real life or in a picture. It followed that television, with all its images of indecently dressed women, was forbidden. At this point, I took my decision.

The study circle and the mosque became the axes of my new life and the starting point for my activities with my new friends, who from then on I came to think of as my brothers. I arranged with some of these 'brothers' of my own age to bring a soccer team from my street to play a team from theirs. I arrived a little late at the pitch and ran into one of the members of our team going home in tears. He told me that the team from the other street had refused to let him play against them because he was a Christian. The team from our street then refused to play out of solidarity with our friend. When I met Sheikh Tareq, I complained to him about the behavior of these colleagues of mine from the study circle. Sheikh Tareq told me that God hated to share the heart of the believer with anyone, which is why He says, *Thou shalt not find any people who believe in God and the Last Day who are loving to those who oppose His Messenger, not though they were their fathers, or their sons, or their brothers, or their clan. Those – He has written faith upon their hearts, and He has confirmed them with a Spirit from Himself ... They are the prosperers* (Qur'an 58:22). Likewise, he noted that the Prophet had said in his Farewell Sermon, "All things that pertain to the Days of Ignorance are placed beneath this foot of mine" (Hadith). Similarly, the Companion of the Prophet Mus'ab ibn Umayr, after he made the migration from Mecca to Medina, had received a visit from someone who told him, "Your mother will neither eat nor drink until you return to her" and he replied by telling the man to tell her that "Mus'ab says, 'Mother, should you have seventy lives and should you depart each life one after the other, I would not abandon this matter.'" I had, therefore, to cut off all relationships with those who did not believe with true faith in God and His Messenger and disdain them, for this was a characteristic of the believers who loved God and whom God loved. If we did not do so, *God would assuredly bring a people He loves and who love Him, humble towards the believers, disdainful towards the unbelievers,* as the Almighty says (Qur'an 5:54).

If learning how to distinguish between what was forbidden and what was permitted was my first lesson in faith, learning how to distinguish oneself from the unbeliever was my first lesson in its practical application. For 'Umar came to the Prophet, God bless him and give him peace, and said, 'O Messenger of God, I went to visit a brother of mine from the tribe of Qurayza and he wrote down for me some concise excerpts from the Torah. Shall I not read them out to you?' At this, the face of the Messenger, God bless him and give him peace, darkened, so Umar said, 'We are content with God as our lord, with Islam as our religion, and with Muhammad as a messenger.' Then the good spirits of the Messenger, God bless him and give him peace, were restored, and he said, 'By Him in whose hand the soul of Muhammad is held, should Musa find himself amongst you and you should follow him, you would go astray! You are my lot amongst the nations, and I am your lot amongst the prophets'" (Hadith). And in his book *Maʿalim fi-l-tariq* (Landmarks on the Road), Sayyid Qutb takes this saying of the Prophet's as his starting point for a proof that there are to be no compromises and no accommodations between Islam and other beliefs – "either Islam or Ignorance" – and to make the claim that this concept of the clear distinction between Islam and Ignorance, insisted upon by the Messenger, was what created that unique, Qurʾanic generation of the first Companions.

When anyone takes his first steps in the Jamaʿa, he cannot tell where the path begins or at what point he will find himself fully committed; everything flows seamlessly. The study circles do not discuss how to confront society, or how the state should be governed. They discuss what is forbidden and what is permitted, they discuss prayer, the rules governing fasting, the rules governing how to look at a woman and listen to music, the limits to be placed on the exposure of the body, the acts that render ritual ablutions void and those that require the ritual purification of the whole body, the proprieties to be observed when bathing and when eating. These are all uncontroversial matters that neither stir suspicion nor sow the seeds of unease. One may respond to any member of one's family who asks, "What did you study today at the mosque?" with complete honesty. In your hand you have a sticker that you put up that says, "I seek refuge with God from all things offensive," this being the prayer to be uttered on entering the bathroom. You also have in your hand another sticker that you put on the front door: "Dear God, let me enter in truthfulness and leave in truthfulness." *Glory be to God who subjected this to us, and we ourselves were not equal to it; surely unto our Lord we are turning* (Qurʾan 43:13–14) is the prayer for mounting a *dabba*, which is the Islamic term for anything that is ridden, from a donkey to a space rocket via motorcycles and cars. I stuck mine on my bike.

These are little things, which, however, when placed one on top of the other, turn into a structure that can stand on its own. On the one hand, there were customs I'd been familiar with and raised in. On the other, there was a new person who, each time he opened his mouth to utter a prayer, felt that he was growing closer to God and that a fine silken thread connected him to the sublime – a thread that tugged at his heart whenever he forgot a prayer, making him remember and say it. Then that tug would disappear and the remembrance would disappear and everything would turn into a mechanical activity. I'd enter the mosque and remove my shoes and leave it and put them on again. I'd say the prayer for leaving the mosque and when I got home, I'd say the prayer for entering the house, and it was the same when I entered the bathroom, where I would use my left hand only to clean myself and not say a word, even if someone called to me. Nor would I forget the prayer when I came out. I ate sitting on the ground using three fingers and not two like the overly dainty or five like those with revolting manners. I didn't ask – especially when eating with the brothers – for a spoon, like someone who put on airs. Even when walking down the street, I would try to walk as the Best of Creation, peace be upon him, was described as having walked, it being said that he did so "as though descending from a high mountain," which meant that I mustn't saunter along slowly. When I thanked someone, I would say, "God bless you" or "God reward you," not "Thanks," as I had been used to doing, or "Merci," as they sometimes say in Egypt. When I spoke, I would articulate the letters clearly, as I had been taught to do when reciting the Qur'an. Instead of pronouncing the name of my friend Diya' with the stress on the first syllable (Díya), I took to pronouncing it on two levels (Diyá'), giving the 'Di' a round, full sound, and the 'yá" a narrow, thin sound, and ending with a glottal stop that was given its full value and didn't disappear as it had done in my old way of speaking.

All this was acceptable. I prayed, I fasted, and I learned the Qur'an. Who could object to that? I did all these things without thinking of myself as a member of the Jama'a Islamiya. I didn't believe that I'd already started down the road.

✳

We hadn't been playing soccer in the street where my house stood for long when one of the players kicked the ball and hit a man who was passing. The man, who was a Christian, picked up the ball and refused to give it back. The player who'd kicked the ball went over to him, apologizing, and asked for it back, but the man swore at him, saying, "God damn your religion!" I don't know how the story reached Brother Husni, but on the evening of the same day he invited me over and asked me to tell him what had happened. He wanted to make sure he had got the facts straight by hearing them from more than one source. The next day, another brother invited me over again and asked me to go with three of the brothers and point out to them the house of the man who had insulted our colleague's religion, and I did so. He then asked me to go up to the man's apartment, which was on the third floor, and inform him that some people wanted to talk to him. I did so and came down again. I heard the brother who was the leader talking to the man from the ground floor and I continued my way out of the building onto the street and stopped some distance away. This brother was waiting for the man at the entrance to the building while the other two stood in front of the building opposite. One of them was the same brother whom I'd seen earlier removing the nail of his whitlowed toe with a knife. When the man came down, he looked suspiciously and expectantly at the three individuals, who were all wearing the same type of beard and the same white jallabiya, and immediately, with a show of warmth, shook the first by the hand, insisting that he get them all something cold to drink. The residents of the man's building and his relatives started coming out onto their balconies. Then two of his male relatives came down to him, the brothers maintaining their refusal of the offer of a cold drink, the three bottles of Coca-Cola being left quietly on the roof of a car next to which the leading brother was talking to the man. From where I was standing, I couldn't hear exactly what they were saying but the conversation was tense and vehement on the part of the leader, while the other man made placatory gestures accompanied by unsuccessful attempts to kiss the brother's head.

The lead brother yelled, "God is great!," the Coca-Cola bottles fell off the top of the car, and the other two brothers rushed over from the opposite building, each carrying his bicycle and each in a split second penning one of the man's two relatives in between wall and bicycle. The man at the center of the quarrel was taken care of by the lead brother.

The cry of "God is great!," the sound of the breaking glass, and the screams of the women from the balconies forced me forward and I ran and kept running in the opposite direction until I reached our house, which was about a hundred meters away, and went up to the roof and hid myself there in an empty room. I thought that to hide in the apartment would be a mistake, as the police would, without a doubt, be coming to arrest me. I was the one who'd gone up to the man's apartment and then stood in the street during the moments preceding the fight. Lots of people must have seen me and lots of people must know who I was since I lived close to the field of battle. I stayed on the roof for hours, monitoring the street and watching for the arrival of the police cars. I didn't come down for the sunset or the evening prayers. Then I went to our apartment, and I did not leave for two days.

I felt repulsion and disgust at what had happened, or perhaps at myself. I had never practiced physical violence, and I was sure in my heart of hearts that the man hadn't given any thought to what my friends' religion was before he cursed it – it was just habit. Even when I was questioned by the brothers about what had happened I wanted to say that, but I didn't. Maybe I'd never expected that things would go so far, or perhaps I'd wanted to watch, the way one does a scene in a movie. In any case, something within me couldn't accept what had taken place. I'd gone to a school the vast majority of whose students were Christians. Until a few weeks before, most of them had been my friends. Ma Soeur Eugenine had even run into me a very short while before and said hello to me, holding my hand in hers while she told some other sisters, whom I didn't know, about me. There was nothing about my appearance to suggest to her that there *was* anything different about me, and I couldn't bring myself to tell her that there was. How, though, could she not feel it? The very same woman had come to our classroom once when the Islamic Religion teacher was away and taught us in his place; she had made us recite the chapter of the Qur'an called *al-Hadid* (Iron), insisting that we pronounce every word correctly down to the last vowel. There were

Muslims in the same school with me but all my friends, without exception, were Christians. Along with them I'd memorized, and can still remember, a few hymns, and they'd made fun of me for not being able to sing them properly to the right tune. My father too was one of the few people willing to rent to tenants of another religion; at that time, renting out only to those of the same religion was a recent practice in Asyut, one that the Christians landlords were the more careful to observe.

These were the feelings that I described to Sheikh Tareq when we met. It was easier than talking about the fact that I was a coward, as proven by my running away in fear, my terror that the police would come for me, and my wishing that I'd never got to know the Jama'a Islamiya or gone to that place, in case any harm might come to me as a result. Or that I wasn't like the two brothers who'd picked up their bicycles with great nimbleness and pounced on the two men. I hadn't even had the courage to stand and watch the events, or to bear the sound of the screaming and the atmosphere of battle. Was I really such a weak-hearted coward?

During our debate, I told him too that when I was in the Fifth Elementary Class (which was after the events of 1981), my Christian friends had started to avoid me and even deliberately insulted me, and when I asked one of them the reason, he'd told me that it was because of the events in Asyut instigated by the Jama'a Islamiya. I asked him what fault of mine was that, and he answered, "You're all Muslims."

"Yes, we're all Muslims," Sheikh Tareq reaffirmed to me. He also told me that when my friend told me that, he was repeating what he'd heard from his parents or at church. Sheikh Tareq added that the "community of unbelievers" was one: the Christian west supported Jewish Israel because it wanted to destroy the Muslims before they became too strong to break or returned to their religion, thus restoring to themselves their glory and power. He reinforced these words with the unanswerable statement of the Lord of the Worlds, "*Never will the Jews be satisfied with thee, neither the Christians, not till thou followest their religion*" (Qur'an 2:120). Then he informed me that the Christian whom the brothers had disciplined for insulting the religion of the Muslims had come and

apologized and sought a truce, and offered to apologize personally to the boy who'd kicked the ball. "Observe," said Sheikh Tareq,
"how God exalts the Muslims and humiliates the unbelievers!"

✳

Umar ibn al-Khattab said, "Teach your children swimming,
archery, and the riding of horses." Despite having started lessons
as a child, I had totally failed to learn how to swim. Even then,
and despite going to the swimming pool with the brothers at least
once a week, I was still unable to learn. I was thin and sank like a
needle. On the other hand, I had been a skilled bike-rider since I
was a child, and hoped to learn to ride a motorcycle, and this took
the place of learning to ride horses, which was not a skill that was
currently taught.

For thirty-two pounds, I bought an air rifle from the Omar
Effendi department store and took it with me to the soccer pitch
for our weekly match following the dawn prayer on Friday. I tried
it a number of times and couldn't hit a thing. One of the brothers who was an outstanding shot, the same one who was good
at kung fu, discovered that the barrel was bent, only slightly but
still enough to send the pellets off course, and another brother
took it upon himself to go with me to Omar Effendi's. Behind the
employee from whom I'd bought the rifle was the white notice
with its heavy black lettering, celebrated throughout Egypt, which
states, Goods Once Sold Cannot Be Returned or Exchanged. This
was meaningless, however, given the presence of a brother at my
side; indeed, he didn't even point to it but exchanged the gun
for another, whose barrel the brother made sure was straight by
placing it on the glass countertop in all positions to check that it
lay completely flush. I tried it out for real a number of times from
the balcony of our apartment on the second story, firing the pellet
toward the lamppost and hearing the sound – tirrin! – that told
me I'd hit it.

I was standing on the same balcony when I saw, in our other
building, opposite, some boys and girls from the three apartments
that made up the ground floor, one of which was occupied by a

Muslim family, the other two by Christians. They were playing 'fishing.' In this game, two players standing opposite one another throw the ball and try to hit the players in the space between them, the players in the middle having to try to avoid the ball. In order to do this, the girls – two of whom were Muslims and two Christians – would raise their skirts above their knees, which would allow them to jump over the balls that were aimed at them. I knew from past conversations that the intentions of the boys, who were all Christians, were not honorable. They had told me, when we'd been friends, about their attempts to trap the neighbor girls into sex, and I used to look forward from one evening to the next for further details, waiting for their attempts to succeed. If they had done so, it would have helped me do the same with the girls, for at such time, I would 'have something over' them and they wouldn't be able to refuse my advances.

That had been during the days of preparation for the shift to manhood, of plans and traps as we awaited the arrival of puberty. By the time that happened, however, I and all these neighbors of mine had arrived at totally different positions. To that point, I still hadn't ejaculated while sleeping, hadn't seen the thick white fluid. All I'd been able to summon up had been a thin substitute. In fact, part of the nonchalance with which I regarded my commitment to the Jama'a was due to the fact that I wasn't yet *mukallaf*, or obligated to obey the precepts of religion, because I had yet to attain puberty, even if, like my peers, my mind itself swam in a sea of semen. My body was changing and those who had gone before brought glad tidings of the signs: "One day you'll start feeling pain in your nipples"; "You'll feel a desire to smoke." And all this was in addition to the comments of my relatives on my swelling nose and my changing voice. Whenever my photograph was taken for some family occasion, I would scrutinize the area between my legs to find out how it must look these days to others. Was there anything there to show I'd become a man?

Manhood, in my new situation, didn't bring with it a desire to smoke. Such things were signs of the Jahiliya, or Days of Ignorance, a part of the Satanic culture that was luring the Muslims further and further away from the Straight Path. To me, as a committed, scripturalist Muslim, puberty was the dividing line between one's being a fully responsible human being and a child whom even God exempted from judgment and who, if he died, would go straight to Heaven. On reaching puberty, not only would I enter the world of men, I would also enter that of those to each of whom God had assigned an angel on his right shoulder, who recorded in writing his good deeds both great and small, and another on his left, who recorded his bad. What a time for the angel of the left to begin his work! I feel for the exhaustion he must have experienced; he was like a policeman starting work on the feast day of Saint Sin. What is it about ejaculation that merits so much attention? I mean, what is it that happens in our bodies, minds, and understanding that merits our transfer to real life in God's eyes? Those boys and girls in the opposite building who were pretending simply to be passing time playing 'fishing' knew as well as I did that they were in fact preoccupied with the roles they were destined to play. I could feel it as I looked at the legs of the girls that were revealed when their household frocks rode up. Indeed, I wanted it the way the worm wants the apple, the way a ticklish throat wants something velvety and moist to spread over it. Now, however, what offended God had to offend me too. True, I might like it, I might long for it. The difference between me and them, however, was that I could gain ascendancy over my body and force theirs to submit to my author-ity, thus preventing everyone from committing sin and protecting – at the very least – the cleanliness of the bodies of Muslim women and their purity, the purity with which they were born. We were taught, from the time we were little children, that looking at girls' bodies was wrong, and that dealings with women in general were subject to limits, and that in Upper Egypt they describe a well-mannered man by saying that "he never looks a woman in the face." At home, my mother would turn the television off during kissing scenes, even though we were not, at that point, an espe-cially hardline household in matters of purity of religion. And even when my friends and I would get together in childhood and look at one another's sexual organs, or hit one another as a pretext for touching what shouldn't be touched – even then we knew that what we were doing was shameful and we'd hide it. When, at age eleven, I learned that we come into the world as a result of sexual intercourse, I was smitten by a bout of disgust with my parents, and I got into a fight with the older neighbor boy who had told me about it and accused him of wanting to insult me. I had, therefore, to put an end to this blameworthy behavior. I took hold of my rifle and aimed it at the entrance to the building. The second the ball appeared there, I fired off a shot at it. Tirrin! It hit the iron door. Everyone stood rooted to the spot, baffled and bewildered. No one dared to go forward and take the ball till the mother of the Muslim girls arrived. She came forward slowly, looking at me, so I lowered my gun as a sign that I'd let her get the ball out of respect. They'd got the message.

A little while after that, there was a quarrel between one of the Christian girls and one of the Muslim girls. The first said something about the stupidity of the Muslims who'd killed one another in Mecca (in a reference to the events at the Sanctuary of Mecca in 1986 that started with the demonstrations by the Iranian pilgrims), so I fetched one of the brothers and pointed out the house of the Christian girl, knowing very well that she could see me. After a while, her father, who was an army officer, came to our house to complain. My father was furious at my behavior, considering it troublemaking and altogether unacceptable, and he tried to stop me from going to the mosque, because it wasn't a matter of "childish misbehavior" anymore and because he thought it not unlikely that our neighbor would report the matter to the police. For my part, I said, with a rhetorical flourish, "'No laxity when Islam is at stake!'" However, I promised him I wouldn't do it again. In fact, I too was worried about the possibility that my father had mentioned. Manhood brought with it, however, both obligations and inconveniences.

I descended the mosque steps calmly after the prayer, talking to a friend of mine. At the mosque of the Jam'iya Shar'iya – the Jama'a's main mosque in Asyut – the number of worshipers was huge. The school year had started a few weeks earlier, the university students arriving from their hometowns and the students at the schools returning from their vacations. The number was larger than any I'd seen throughout the summer vacation. This was also my first school year as a committed Muslim with the Jama'a; it was First Year Secondary. The atmosphere in the city was tense, for it was one of those times when the government had decided that Islamist activity had gone too far and had to be put a stop to. At such times, the mosque would be surrounded by thousands of Central Security troops, who would prevent some preacher or other from giving his sermon or terrorize those who frequented the mosque in the hope that they would decide not to take the risk of going. The huge number of those attending the prayer could act either as a stimulus to the police to interfere, in an attempt to prevent more people from coming, or as a deterrent. On this occasion, it had been a stimulus. For a moment, I was deprived of speech, as though some power had sucked the words out of my mouth. The buzz of people talking, the sound of their footfalls, the cries of the stall keepers, the attentive expression on my friend's face all froze, and then suddenly everything exploded. Two agitated hands pushed me from behind, feet stepped on the backs of my shoes, dragging them off my feet. Shots were fired in the air and people knocked into one another like ninepins, moving together this way and that as though by prior agreement. Once again I yielded to my instincts and ran away from the shooting, but the roaring of the Central Security soldiers and the deafening sound of thousands of feet pounding the ground to an irregular rhythm started coming from all sides and I didn't know which way to turn. An acrid smoke that got into the nostrils was added to the atmosphere's other ingredients. One's entire face was afflicted with a burning sensation that would stop at one knew not which layer of one's skin; indeed, it didn't seem as though it was going to stop at all, one's whole body apparently bursting into flame in an instant, just as every atom of the air around me had taken fire all at one go. I had the feeling that our house existed in a different world, one separated from me by frightful obstacles. I would run like a madman and enter a building, then retreat and flee again when the residents refused to open their doors and give us refuge. There seemed no escape from the torment that the police, who now filled the place, would inflict on us with their thick, electrified batons. I went on running from street to street and from thorough-fare to thoroughfare, forgetting that my age, which was still under fifteen, and my face, on which neither beard nor mustache had yet sprouted, would be enough to hide me from notice so long as I walked normally. The brother who had gone with me to change the shotgun stood, holding high a crutch belonging to a brother who was a cripple and sold perfumes in front of the Jam'iya Shar'iya mosque and yelled in the face of the fleeing people, "Stand firm: your religion is under attack! Defend your Islam!"

I saved the scene in my memory but wasn't strong enough to answer his call. Indeed, I kept running till I reached our house, where the windows were closed tight to stop the tear gas from the grenades. Through the slanting wooden slats of the shutters I could see the final moments of the battle. The security forces dispersed the people and began chasing those who couldn't run fast enough to get away, beating them viciously while herding them toward the large security trucks. My tears weren't because of the gas now. I went to my bed and lay down on my back in the darkened room. I remembered the movies that depicted the first Muslims and their confrontations with the tyranny of the unbe-lievers. I fell asleep before my tears had dried.

I found myself in a dark, deserted place divided equally into narrow paths that all came together at a circle in the middle. Pre-cisely at the center stood a white dog, which was barking. I was extremely frightened of dogs, and this dog was barring my return route. I looked all around in the hope of finding a path that would allow me to avoid the dog but I couldn't find one. I felt a crip-pling fear in my legs. I couldn't move. I could see that the only light on that dark path was on the other side but I didn't have the courage to walk past the dog and get to it. I gathered all my strength and walked on, trembling, impelled only by the certainty that I would perish if I didn't do so. I walked toward the dog, has-tening my steps as I said in a loud voice, recalling a song we sang at the mosque, "No, we shall not die cringing for fear of the dogs. No, we shall not die cringing for fear of the dogs."

I woke from my dream still weeping.

✳

I still considered myself no more than a sympathizer with the Jama'a. I wasn't a member and I didn't want to be one. I was still a child – or such was my unchanging image of myself. Nobody had the right to punish me or take what I did seriously. In fact, the whole world wasn't supposed to be that serious. There was still plenty of time left for one to stop and turn back from a game that was played with the nonchalance, the mindset, and the innocence of a child. I myself didn't take what I was doing seriously. When I joined First Year Secondary, which was my first year with the Jama'a Islamiya as well, I talked a lot with my friends about the Jama'a, but without real interest. Talking to us about the early days of Islam, the History teacher would say that the army of Abraha the Abyssinian had attacked Mecca but that strong winds had driven him back. With a mixture of rowdiness and provocation, I would stand up with theatrical flourish and say, *"Nay! God loosed against them birds in flights, hurling against them stones of baked clay, and He made them like green blades devoured!"* (Qur'an 105:3). Then I would sit down, laughing, and the teacher, who was a Christian, wouldn't dare to strike me but would satisfy himself with giving me a dirty look. I was joking but I also had a message: how could people like him challenge the word of the Lord of the Worlds, and was this not a part of the conspiracy that was being hatched against Islam? Sometimes I would joke around for no reason at all. The Math teacher would be explaining his lesson and I'd stick my head out from my desk, look toward the door, and pretend that I was talking to someone there. The man would stop in the middle of his lesson and turn toward the door to see who it was and find no one. It never occurred to me that the matter was anything more than a joke.

At the start of 1987, pamphlets were distributed calling on Muslims to refrain from celebrating the Christian new year, since to do so was akin to unbelief. "He who resembles a people becomes one of their number, and he who spends much time with them shall be marshaled with them on the Day of Judgment," said the

Prophet. I had nothing to do with the pamphlet. I was still avoiding, even at that point, any organized activism, not to mention that the pamphlet was put out by the Muslim Brotherhood, not the Jamaʿa Islamiya to which I 'belonged.' It happened, however, that a meeting of the school's Parents' Association was subjected to a tirade by the father of one of my fellow students, a professor at the Faculty of Agriculture who had obtained his doctorate in Germany, because the school had permitted the distribution of such pamphlets to the students, including his son. The university professor also said that I was among those who had distributed the pamphlets. This was the first time my name had been brought up in an official context. Afterward, the principal called me in and gave me a warning.

They were right about one thing: this business was no joke. How could one joke when the Lands of Islam were witnessing what they were? In the summer of 1987, I started going to movies shown by the Jamaʿa at the Jamʿiya Sharʿiya mosque. There were pictures of children disfigured during the war against the Muslims in Afghanistan that would have wrung tears from a stone, while the rallying songs in the background stirred up one's anger, and the thunderous voice of the narrator poured scorn on those who abandoned their brother Muslims and left them prey to the unbelievers, mocking the 'civilization' that the equally unbelieving west and east made so much fuss over, and recounting the miracles that God had performed at the hands of the holy warriors. The events depicted in the movie were intercut in quick succession with the image of an old man with a thick white beard, wrinkled face, and piercing eyes, a Kalashnikov hanging from his shoulder, climbing a mountain. The camera then slowly descended to dwell on the old man's hands, clasped behind his back, fingers toying calmly with a dangling string of prayer beads. Scenes of confrontations in various places followed one another and ended with the image of a stone in the hand of a young warrior, a child younger than me. The child threw the stone into the air and the camera followed it in slow motion till it fell on a Russian tank, which exploded as the voice of a singer arose behind the flames:

With this the fire is kindled.
Onward, then, defenders!
The winds of Paradise are blowing.
Happy then, you martyrs!

Can any extinguish such a fire?
Who will tend it night and day?
Who will protect our honor,
From the tyrant's wanton sway?

Our nation is not of the east
Nor of the lands of the west.
Our nation is Islamic.
Come, make it once more blest!

I had full confidence in those who were ready to take up the
challenge, those who were capable, with their honesty, their self-
sacrifice, and their faith, of reviving this nation. They were the
ones whom I played soccer with and prayed with, and at whose
hands I studied. They were the ones who, when I was in their
midst, made me feel safe and protected, the ones who, should I fail
to show up, would ask about me, as though my mere absence was
an event of significance. These brothers gave me, to increase me in
my faith, a sticker on which was drawn the globe with, around it,
the Qur'anic promise, *"God has promised those of you who believe
and do righteous deeds that He will surely make you successors in
the land, even as He made those of you who were before them successors, and that He will surely establish their religion for them that
He has approved for them, and will give them in exchange, after
their fear, security: 'They shall serve Me, not associating with Me
anything'"* (Qur'an 24:55). I stuck it on the door.

Even though I left these movies full of zeal and of a desire to
take revenge on those who had abandoned the Muslims to their
fate and whom concern for their religion had failed to motivate to
go to their aid, I felt that expressing sympathy and weeping tears
of sorrow over the victims were as far as I could go. I still felt that
I was constrained by the limits of my tall, thin body, constrained

by the walls of our apartment, constrained by the walls of fear. I also felt that I was constrained geographically, that I would never see the events that were taking place in those distant lands, and that they would never see me. One day, however, as I was leaving the Jam'iya Shar'iya mosque, a brother I didn't know came up to me and asked me if I would mind staying by the books that he sold by the mosque wall so that he could go in and perform the prayer. I sat down next to the box of books and took a look at one of them. It turned out to be a booklet published by the Jama'a Islamiya that bore the title *Hatmiyat al-muwajaha* (The Inevitability of Confrontation). The book spoke, as its title indicated, of military confrontation with the secular Egyptian regime as the sole means for the extension of the dominion of God's religion over the Earth. In support of its arguments, the book adduced (in addition to the arguments of the jurisprudents) practical evidence that demonstrated that no political appeal had ever, over the course of history, had any success with repressive regimes such as that of Egypt. By way of example, it pointed to the movements of the Muslim Brotherhood in Egypt and the Refah Party in Turkey, the leader of which, Necmettin Erbakan, had been banned to prevent him from taking power.

As I was ignorant of the contents of the book when I agreed to sit beside the box, I satisfied myself with telling those who asked about its contents, "Look at what's written on the back cover and you'll find out." My response was an attempt on my part to maintain a distance between me and the book – I'd read the back cover before people asked me about it, so I understood what it contained. As time passed, however, I started leafing through it so as to be able to give a better answer. Not long had passed before I felt that the book somehow belonged to me, as I was the one selling it to people now, and that selling it, despite all the weighty and important ideas that it contained, was easy and straightforward, not much different from selling collections of children's books and adventure stories or light fiction. My heart lost its fear of everything that related to government, *hakimiya* (or God's right to govern), and armed confrontation. I took a copy home with me to read and of course it raised a number of issues that the study circle started to deal with. Islamist rulings on jihad and *hisba* ("the commanding of good and the forbidding of evil") were added to what we were already studying in these sessions and treated on the same footing as the jurisprudence on prayer, fasting, and alms giving. We also started studying the thinking of other Islamist movements, especially the Muslim Brotherhood, the Takfir wa-l-Hijra (the Movement for the Attribution of Unbelief and Migration), the Tawaqquf wa-l-Tabyin (the Movement for Scrutiny and Discrimination), and the Ansar al-Sunna (the Partisans of the Sunna). These lessons focused in the first place on the religious errors into which these groups had fallen, and then turned to the study of their tactical errors, which were attributed to their breaking of Islamic law.

By way of example, the Muslim Brotherhood had committed the jurisprudential error of participating in the elections to the People's Council, or parliament, which was the most extreme manifestation of unbelief in Egypt because it deprived God of His absolute right to legislate for humankind and awarded it to a group of mortals. This major error had, moreover, led to a tactical error on the part of the Brotherhood as a movement in that they thus participated in beautifying the face of the secular regime in Egypt by making it appear open to all ideas and currents, provided these worked within the system. This gave the regime the necessary justification for striking at other Islamist movements that refused to join the fake democratic system. Historically, the experience of the Brotherhood demonstrated that the regime, having once taken care of the currents that constituted a threat to it, would turn on them and deal with them just as it had with the others.

The Ansar al-Sunna, on the other hand, were simply "plowing water" since they concentrated on proselytization and excluded jihad, and whatever this group might accomplish in a year, the "organs of license and depravity" (otherwise known as the organs of the media) would demolish in a day. Things were different with regard to the Takfir wa-l-Hijra and the Tawaqquf wa-l-Tabyin movements, for these had been distracted by their preoccupation with delving into people's degrees of faith and scrutinizing their hearts, and when they ended up deciding that the whole society was in a state of unbelief had cut themselves off from it and made no effort to change it. Only the Jama'a Islamiya raised the Qur'an in one hand and the sword in the other, proselytizing, practicing jihad, and also "commanding good and forbidding evil." It followed that, as stated in the *Mithaq al-'amal al-islami* (The Islamic Action Charter), which constituted the Jama'a's constitution, "our own path consists of calling people to God, commanding good and forbidding evil, and struggling for God through a grouping whose actions are governed by the True Law, that rejects hypocrisy and inaction, and that has learned from earlier experiences."

The Inevitability of Confrontation, The Islamic Action Charter, and Landmarks on the Road are the three books with which my new Islamist culture began. They took the place of the novels of Agatha Christie that I'd started reading at age eleven as a natural progression from children's adventure stories. However, the weighty ideas they contained concerning the necessity for the total separation of the program of change adopted by us as Islamists from that which the secularist regimes sought to impose on us were not presented to us in this dry way. There are easier roads to the heart's acceptance, means that take one far from the fever of the rites and practices of religion and the woodenness of words. Such things are more easily digested when taken in the form of songs, such as those sung by a brother with an Upper Egyptian accent about the students who had come to the city to study only to be taken by surprise by the sinful behavior that was everywhere there:

"Police," we asked, "does it please you that oppression is our due
While unbelief weaves its web and fills the city's streets?"
Said they, "We do what we are told to do."

We said, "By God, neither exhortation nor guidance is a cure.
Their hearts are evil. Only jihad will do.
Strike, Zuhdi, strike. Cleanse through us the land and make it pure."

One by one their castles fall, tho' their soldiers like locusts the
    land consume.
Let this be a lesson for every tyrant, till the Day of Doom.

First performed as a song, such words are soon transformed into emotional energy, filling people's souls and bodies and becoming an incontrovertible truth: neither exhortation nor guidance is a cure; their hearts are evil. Only jihad will do.

2

God is mine alone

The Rahma Mosque was the Jama'a Islamiya's second largest. It was closer to our house than their main mosque, that of the Jam'iya Shar'iya, and contained a spacious prayer hall for men. In addition to the main entrance, off which were the bathrooms and the facilities for ritual ablution, there was another entrance, which joined the main room to a patio that would also be spread with reed mats for the Friday prayer. This patio was surrounded by a concrete wall and had its own steps. The interior walls were a light cream and the floor was covered with a darker carpet, of a shade of brown that could withstand the large number of wet feet that trod it every day, retaining from this wetting a certain dampness that softened the heat of the air when one was seated on it. The fans suspended from the high ceiling also created deflected breezes that made the air inside the place agreeable, especially at midday in the summer. Because the members of the Jama'a were familiar with the Jam'iya Shar'iya mosque and frequented it more, the Rahma Mosque provided greater privacy. By the same token, praying there reduced the amount of time I spent in idle chat afterward and spared me having to argue with my parents about spending most of my time outside the house at the expense of my studies. During the summer vacation, I would spend the time between my noon and my afternoon prayers there, most often alone or with friends of mine whom I had already known well even before we had become committed to the Jama'a. I would read the Qur'an, or read a book, or pass the time chatting with them, or even take a nap, without anyone disturbing me and without being under the eyes of the plainclothes detectives who usually surrounded the Jam'iya Shar'iya mosque. When the time for the next prayer came, I would turn on the loudspeakers and give the call to prayer. When the time for the call to prayer found me at home, I'd keep an ear cocked to make sure that the call was in fact to be heard emanating from the Rahma Mosque. Sometimes it was not, in which case I would hurry over from the house on my bicycle and in three minutes be giving the call. I knew everyone who went to the Rahma Mosque, even those who weren't brothers, because they all lived close by. Only very rarely did anyone whom I didn't know come to the mosque. This man was one such.

He sat next to me, wearing thick glasses, his face lined not from advancing years but with the sort of wrinkles that seem to come from intense thought. He asked me what I thought of the society we were living in, and whether we ought to excuse people because of their ignorance or declare them unbelievers because they did not practice an appropriate awareness of the oneness of God. I dredged up from the back of my mind the information I'd gathered on the subject over the past years and said, "The former." In support of this position, I cited two Qur'anic verses: "*We never chastise, until We send forth a Messenger*" (17:15) and "*The Lord would never destroy the cities unjustly, while their inhabitants were heedless*" (6:131).

I thought the proof was clear, in that God would never chastise people until He had sent them a messenger. Religious discussions – debates over the fine points of the Truth – are never that simple, however. The man said that God had indeed sent a messenger, had sent in fact the Seal of All Messengers, after whom no other messenger would be sent. I replied that 'messenger' here was used in a figurative sense and meant anyone who could teach the people. The man smiled. He took hold of his ear lobe and pulled it downward, his expression transformed into one of willing piety, as of one who conjures up the spirits of the dead. He told me, "Hear the words of God Almighty in the chapter of the Qur'an called al-A'raf (The Battlements), which seem to be addressed to us today, as though he were speaking directly to us" (and here he started chanting in the style used when reciting from the Qur'an during prayers): "*And when thy Lord took from the Children of Adam, from their loins, their seed, and made them testify touching themselves, 'Am I not your Lord?' they said, 'Yes, we testify'* – lest you should

say on the Day of Resurrection, 'As for us, we were heedless of this,'
or lest you say, 'Our fathers were idolaters aforetime, and we were
seed after them. What, wilt Thou then destroy us for the deeds of the
vain-doers?'" (Qur'an 7:172).

I didn't know what to say, for I hadn't memorized the Qur'an as
well as he had. In reality, I knew nothing, and over the past year
since I had got to know the brothers, the subject had not been
raised in earnest. We knew the Jama'a's position and we followed
it, but we didn't know the proofs for it. Even more importantly,
we hadn't studied the proofs cited by those who differed with that
position, and couldn't refute them. At the same time, the chanting
of the Qur'an in that voice full of submission and with that face
inscribed with fear and awe that I myself could feel conjured up
before my very eyes the embodiment of faith. In fact, I could even
see the spermatozoa that I'd studied in Third Preparatory. I could
see them standing in their millions from before the beginning of
time in front of a figure of universal power, their tails trembling,
their featureless heads speaking and bearing testimony to their
faith. Where was I among those vast throngs? I was there with
them. Thus stated our Book, of which the Qur'an says that *false-*
hood comes not to it from before it nor from behind it (41:42). Few,
though, were those who kept faith with this covenant. Few were
those who remembered that trembling and the fear and dread of
that awe-filled scene. Was I one of them? And why should I be and
others not? There were things inside us that we could not comprehend. We might grasp them by accident or discover a meager part
of them according to our limited capacities to comprehend, but
they were engraved within us. If it were not so, how could I and
he and the committed brothers have stayed true to the covenant
while others did not? The man's voice as he chanted the Qur'an
was insistent. It probed the depths and reached the essential part
of a man's soul. At the same time, though, it created doubt – doubt
in oneself and in where one stood with regard to the infinity of all
that had gone before. The wonderful, artistic image was terrifying,
and that fideistic lottery was as far as could be from reassuring
one or encouraging him to feel at ease as to his destiny. The Commander of the Faithful, Umar ibn al-Khattab, God rest his soul,

said, "If one of my feet were in Paradise and the other outside of it, I could not guarantee God's judgment of me." The divine truth was very, very precise, and those who had insight into it and followed it were a tiny, tiny band. And who were they anyway, given that everyone believed, and had faith and confidence that they were in the right?

Since I had got to know the brothers, the thing I loved most and that brought me the greatest peace of mind was the Hadith of the Prophet (pbuh) that described the 'strangers' as those people who held fast to the true faith at a time when "holding on to one's religion was like holding on to a burning ember" (Hadith). On my books, there were stickers with the first Hadith that I had heard and memorized: "Islam began as a stranger and it will once more be a stranger as it began; so blessed are the strangers." This was the Hadith as it appeared on the sticker. However, some authorities related it with additions: "It was said, 'O Messenger of God, and who are "the strangers?"' He said, 'A small group among a large number of evil people. Those who disobey them are more than those who obey them.'" In another version it says that they are "those plucked from among the tribes," and in yet another it says that they are "those who restore to its correct form that part of my sunna that people have corrupted." All these characteristics could be applied to me and to my brothers, for we were individuals from different places and families and we were correcting that part of the sunna of the Prophet (pbuh) that people had corrupted. We had given new life to the Prophet's habit of using an aromatic twig to clean his teeth, his way of growing his beard, and so on. And we were, naturally, a small group among a large number of evil people, and we were obeyed by far fewer than we were disobeyed by.

But why should this man, who retained that awesome ancient scene still in his memory, who had not ceased to give evidence of his submission, and who trembled whenever he recalled it – why shouldn't this man and his group be the ones in the right? Perhaps they were the true strangers, because they were even fewer than us and more stringent in matters of creed. Perhaps, if one thought about it, one might discover that he was correct.

Brother Ahmad Abduh emerged into the light from the side room that was next to the ablution facilities. He was the Supreme Amir of the Jama'a Islamiya in Asyut. He had piercing eyes that looked out from behind the thick glasses that are worn by all doctors after their early thirties. Like any leader to whom nature has granted distinctive characteristics on all levels, he had a slight limp and favored his left leg. Even when you couldn't see him, his high-pitched voice was distinguishable from everyone else's, for he spoke fast and swallowed his letters so that you could only make out what he was saying when you were close to his dark, black-bearded face and listened with absolute concentration. His mustache was either shaved off completely or clipped down to a very few hairs spread out along the broad gray line beneath his nose, so that they looked like thorns sprouting from bare earth. His two front teeth stuck out and weren't completely covered even when he closed his lips. Catching sight of us, he looked at me angrily, sent me away, and spoke to the man for five minutes, not more. Then he came over and forbade me to talk to heretics unless there was someone with me who was more knowledgeable than I who could refute their invalid arguments. If the truth were comprehensible through the exercise of my meager store of knowledge, everything would be easy, and if we were to try to comprehend the truth with our minds, we would lose our religion and its rules, or, in the words of the old expression, "If religion could be seized by the mind, the underside of the footwear would be wiped and not the top." (When the Muslim repeats his ritual ablutions and is wearing socks that he donned when in a state of ritual purity, he wipes the top side of the sock with water. If he were to exercise his mental capacities, he would wipe the underside, which comes into contact with the ground and to which dirt may attach itself. By so doing, however, he would contravene the religious rule.)

On another occasion, I sat down next to a man from the Fara-mawi group. Later I learned from the brothers that its members do not believe in the Prophetic Hadiths at all. In fact, they consider these invalid as a source for religious lawmaking, on the grounds that the Prophet himself forbade people to record them and that, given the elapse of time, there was no guarantee that they were transmitted accurately, for various reasons, starting with human error and forgetfulness and ending with the surreptitious introduction of false Hadiths by the enemies of Islam.

Worse than any of these groups was the Muslim Brotherhood. This was the group with whose followers – impostors who wore the robe of Islam while gnawing at its body – we above all clashed. Our brothers in the university would prevent them, by force if necessary, from distributing those pamphlets of theirs in which they would extol falsehood and which they would then sign with the name of the Jama'a Islamiya. They were, as a senior brother told me, with some exaggeration, "worse for Islam than the Jews." At school, we would get into fierce arguments with them. One day, the brothers told us that we would pray the evening prayer at the mosque of Abu al-Jud, the Muslim Brotherhood mosque in Asyut, so I went, not knowing why. I prayed the evening prayer and listened to a homily delivered by a member of the rival group, my eyes roaming as I made a count of the brothers from my group whom I knew and searching for anything unusual that might explain our presence there. Nothing happened, and we left. I asked one of the brothers why we had gone and he told me that the Brotherhood member who had preached, Esam el-Eryan, was given to claiming that he was the founder of the Jama'a Islamiya, and we had gone there to answer him back, should he do so. "Mightn't that have led to a fight?" I asked. "So what?" said the brother. "We were prepared." The dispute over who owned the copyright on a name so full of associations as that of the Jama'a Islamiya was not something to be taken lightly.

Until such time as you should attain enough knowledge to enable you to grasp the divine truth, the pious thing to do is to leave such matters up to the home team and not worry about what others said, or, to put it another way, to accept the group that God had seen fit to assign you to; otherwise you'd be changing groups every week. I had no desire to change. I loved the brothers. To me, they were an extended family, one chosen by God, and not just kinfolk imposed upon one. All of us used 'brother' as a term of address, even if the rank of the one addressed was a bit higher, such as those known as 'Sheikh, who combined all the elements of fatherhood, including its harshness, its tenderness, its knowledge, and its care, and those known as 'Mawlana' (Master), which was a term we could use of anyone but which was reserved mostly for the older brothers and added to feelings of love and familial relationship those of protection and support, of being marshaled under the same divine banner as the angels, the Messenger, and the believers, old and new, and even of God Himself: *God is his protector, and Gabriel, and the righteous among the believers* (Qur'an 66:4). In this group of ours, we would not keep a quarrel going for more than three days because to do so was forbidden by religion, and if we got into a quarrel, there was an authority that would judge justly between us. We loved one another 'in God' as evidence of divine intervention: "The souls of men are as soldiers under God's command – those that draw close to one another live in harmony with one another and those that draw apart from one another are at variance with one another," as the Messenger (pbuh) said. And if we were to 'fall in love with one another in God' without previously having been acquainted, we would express our love openly to one another. Thus, one of us might go up to a man whom he felt he loved for no reason and tell him, "So and so, I love you in God" and the beloved would reply, "May God, in whom you love me, love you." Such couples who 'loved one another in God' were guaranteed a place among "the seven [whom] God will protect with his shadow on the day when there is no shadow but His." Among such, according to the text of the Hadith, were "two men who love one another in God, who came together through Him and were separated through Him."

That summer, I went to my father's village and relived the atmosphere that I loved there, among my cousins, in my biological extended family in its Big House. We would play soccer from morning to night, then sit and listen to tales of jinn and afreets under the night's shining stars. This annual journey of mine to my father's village had been the joy of my life since I was young. As our family lived 400 kilometers south of Cairo, which put us about 650 kilometers from Alexandria, we never ever went to that resort city to swim in the sea like other people. The trip to the village was our summer holiday. It was the one place where I'd agree to eat fish, and relish greens such as Jews' mallow, which I'd mix with rice while my mother looked on in wonder and reproached me for not doing the same at home in Asyut. Everything about the village, from fishing in the waters of the canal with a primitive fishing rod to knocking dates off the palm trees with stones to riding the open pickup trucks and walking behind the camel that bore the green covering of the tomb belonging to Hajj Salim el-Arabi, miracle-worker and master of portents and punishments (a practice that I now discovered from the Jama'a was a form of polytheism), represented for me a magical world of special significance.

I extended my stay in the village for weeks. I had the time to find out where I wanted to be. I decided, as I lay on the couch in the television room of the Big House, that I didn't want this life with the brothers. The pace of my close association with them was increasing in such a way as to shift the matter, with all its weighty implications, from the realm of jest to that of seriousness, and I didn't want that. Immediately, however, I felt fear, a fear of loss such as I had felt only once before, when my mother had wanted a divorce. That day, my father had phoned my aunt on my mother's side and her husband, who had raised her after her mother had died at about the same age (nine) that I was then and her father had remarried, and asked them to persuade her to abandon her decision. I stood behind the door in my room, listening to the conversation, fearing what it might lead to. I felt at the time that I was a postulate in an equation that I had no input into, that I was merely a number in a calculation, but that I would bear a share of the cost in whatever way my mother's relatives might determine in the light of their greater experience of life. The problem blew over and the divorce never took place. Today, my fear of loss was different because I was the one who was taking the decision and I was the one who would pay the full price. How often my brethren had warned me against being away from them, as it is "the stray lamb that gets eaten by the wolf." Brother Husni had told Sheikh Mahmud, in my hearing, that he had gone to visit a brother who had been with them in prison following the killing of Sadat and who following his release had become so preoccupied with his business affairs, that, during the visit, the bearded brother had held his glass of tea "with his left hand, God forbid!"

I turned onto my right side, then my left. I spat to my left three times. The thoughts going round in my head must, without a doubt, be the work of the Devil, who whispers to men to take the easy road in this world and let slip the eternal ease that resides in the next, inflating to him the pleasures of this life until he imagines that he will never be able to live without them. In a year, I would be sixteen years old, the same age as Usama ibn Zayd when he assumed command of the Muslim army at the last battle for which the Prophet himself had laid the plans, and here I was, thinking like a child about playing soccer and fishing. I decided to cut short my holiday and return to Asyut, for there could be no life without my brothers. The one I loved most among them, Sheikh Mahmud Shu'eib, was only three years older than me when he went to prison in connection with the killing of Sadat. He spent three continuous years there and since his release he hadn't spent a single night at home. Barely a month would pass between one detention and the next, but he would emerge each time more unyielding than before; a true hero, and yet modest as well. He'd be brought a glass of tea as I was sitting with him and ask me to put my finger in it to make it sweeter. He was an eloquent preacher, whose words seemed to summon up spontaneously rain, lightning, thunder, swords, spring and its colors. In minutes they could make your body grow as hot as a chair that had been sitting in the sun for hours, or in an instant be stirred as though it had been set ablaze by the sight of crimson blood. Then from this heat and turmoil they would transport you to the cold of a winter cloud or the gentle caress of summer's shade. Despite this, he would come to me sometimes and ask me about the correct ending for a word in Classical Arabic and whether he had made any grammatical mistakes in his sermon. We'd be in the middle of the throngs in the mosque and when the preacher made a grammatical mistake, his eyes would search me out in the crowd and he'd smile – "You and I know what he did."

And again, I asked myself, what would it mean if you gave up your tapes of Abd el-Halim Hafez, on whose songs you were raised, whether from the radio playing in the kitchen or from your mother's mouth as she prepared the food? What would it mean if you gave up watching the television around which the family gathered, the words of whose films you'd memorized, whose plays had inspired your jokes, and which made you shout for joy whenever you saw the soccer team you supported score a goal on its screen; the television that entertained you when you were bored and kept you company from the time you opened your eyes until the moment you closed them? What would it mean if you had to give up exchanging secrets with the friends you'd been raised with? What would it mean if you set aside your dreams of a career, or put them in jeopardy?

It wouldn't mean a thing, I answered myself.

Even if there had been no Jama'a Islamiya, the stories of love that Abd el-Halim Hafez sang were no more than delusions, tales of enchanted fairies. It was sheer foolishness for someone who was never going to hold a girl's hand and look into her eyes under the watchful gaze of a thousand others to listen to such things. The endlessly repeated movies no longer had any flavor; like a newspaper months old read in solitary confinement, the only thing to recommend them was that they reminded you that such things existed. It was better a thousand times over, as the brothers said, to play soccer than to watch it, for to do the latter was to waste one's time, and the professional players wore shorts that showed their 'lesser pudenda' (from the knee to the upper thigh). Tales told by friends within the walls of apartments or the walls of schools were merely a source of torment: no journey would take you to distant places, no activity would brighten your days, and no camps would dig up your hidden talents. Nothing. Nothing. Even your career you had realized long ago was determined by factors you had no control over. When I was in my mother's womb, she'd seen my grandmother in a dream and she'd given her a drake and told her that if it lived it would be without equal. I was born sickly and my parents were afraid I would die. However, I was lucky. God had chosen me from among His slaves for whom he had set aside in perpetuity, in this world and in the next, "a home better than their home and a family better than their family" and I was lucky to have been chosen. I would say to Sheikh Tareq that the brothers had not made their way to me but I had made my way to them, and he would say to me, "So thank the Lord, then!" I would thank Him, but I would also feed my self-conceit: if they – my ignorant peers – had been chosen, they, for their part, would likewise have preferred to be with the Jama'a, which meant that God Himself had without a doubt chosen me, perhaps because I was of a good family whose fortunes had suffered a reverse, perhaps because God had looked into my heart and found in it a love of the good, perhaps because He had looked at me with that satisfaction with which He regards only a limited number of people, who remain unknown to the rest of humankind. Perhaps, perhaps, perhaps. What was certain was that there was something personal about the whole thing – "the blood line extends to the seventh genera-tion." Had not my grandfather's funeral, which I hadn't witnessed, been the largest that my father's village, Kom el-Arab, had ever seen? It wasn't money, which came and went, or influence, which is given to the undeserving, that made men great; it was God's regard and will, which did not grant such things according to this world's criteria but in exchange for a high price that He Himself set. And that high price could not be merely to pray five times a day, fast for a month, and undertake works of supererogation.

My love for the brothers helped me to perceive more clearly the divine truth implanted in my heart. In a situation such as this, however, in which the man was using the Qur'an to prove that there was no excuse for ignorance, it was insufficient. That man also believed that he had grasped the truth, and there can only be one Truth. The brothers took us through a study of the religious sources on the subject, following which we were better acquainted with the religious arguments, and stronger in our belief – *Nay, but We hurl the truth against falsehood and it prevails over it, and behold, falsehood vanishes away* (Qur'an 21:18). Inevitably, from the question concerning the excuse of ignorance rose another: if our group excused people on the grounds of their ignorance, why did it fight them? This question was raised, in this conditional for-mulation, by the Muslim Brotherhood. The study entitled *Qital al-ta'ifa al-mumtani'a 'an tanfidh hukm min ahkam Allah* (On Fighting Those Who Refuse to Implement a Law of God), which responds to this argument, is one of the most important in the eyes of the Jamaʻa and is, in my opinion, the most important study to have been produced by jihadist thought, for it establishes the shariʻa framework for the most significant differences in conduct between the Jamaʻa and other groups, the Jamaʻa being the only group to combine proselytization with jihad while at the same time not stigmatizing the entire society as unbelieving. The apparent contradiction among these three positions has puzzled sympathizers, critics, and students alike.

"It may be legitimate to fight a person and not to kill him," states the study, killing being restricted to a particular individual who fulfills the justifiable conditions for killing, such as one who fights against God's religion and openly manifests his hostility toward it, in which case the factors that would prohibit his killing, such as ignorance and necessity, have been removed. Only persons of this sort were to be found on the assassination lists. Others, such as members of the Central Security Force, were to be fought because they were the human shield of a regime that refused to implement God's laws, while at the same time these members were acknowledged to be Muslims. This meant that I could not pursue a given individual member of the Central Security Force with the purpose of monitoring his movements and killing him. Fighting a specific group, however, such as the Central Security Force, most of whose foot soldiers were semi-literate villagers, resembled, according to the study, the actions of Abu Bakr al-Siddiq when he fought those who, in the early days of Islam, refused to give alms, even while he acknowledged that they had made the conversion to Islam, and the appropriation of whose womenfolk he did not regard as being permissible under religious law, unlike that of the womenfolk of the unbelievers. To put the matter in a contemporary context, killing resembled the carrying out of a judicial sentence of execution, whereas fighting was an armed uprising against the ruling regime, or a war with another state's regime.

What is notable about fundamentalist studies – and this is no exception – is that they take as their starting point a paraphrase of a passage, which is known as the *matn* (text) and consists, after the manner of the books of the classical canon, of short phrases that contain the main points of the study and are easy to memorize. On many occasions, the text is in rhymed prose, or partially so, or in verse, all these factors helping to keep the points firmly in one's head, even if the details of the proofs adduced should slip one's memory, or one should find them difficult to understand. For this particular study, the text goes, "Any (1) group (2) possessed of strength and the power to resist that (3) refuses to implement (4) a law of God (5) must be fought and (6) disavowed and (7) fighting such a group takes precedence over fighting unbelievers."

Of course, the numbers are mine, supplied to demonstrate the concentrated nature of the phrases of the text. Every term following a number is a subject of one of the lessons of the study.

The study has a strategic aspect too, the writers pointing to the fact that no revolutionary movement in a state with a repressive regime has succeeded in attaining power other than through the use of arms. This part appealed to me greatly, since it was in keeping with my reading of other books that dealt with religion as a political phenomenon of our age, such as *al-Manhaj al-haraki li-l-sira al-nabawiya* (The Strategic Plan of the Prophet's Life History), and likewise with the beginnings of my addiction to the works of Sayyid Qutb. I found pleasing the idea that the Qur'an and the Sunna – or in other words, Islam itself – could be a strategic plan drawn up to show us how to establish our divine state and in so doing push off our chests those who knelt upon them and determined our destinies and those of our countries. The fulfillment was approaching of the promises that God Almighty had made to us: *He will surely establish their religion for them that He has approved for them, and will give them in exchange, after their fear, security* (Qur'an 24:55) and *The truth has come, and falsehood vanished away; surely falsehood is ever certain to vanish* (Qur'an 17:81).

From the Jama'a Islamiya's discipline and its commitment to the truth, from the way the other groups mistook falsehood for truth, from Sayyid Qutb, from love, from hate, from need, and from abnegation, we absorbed God's word, absorbed the shining white message in all its purity and precision, exactly as it had been revealed to the Noble Messenger.

God's message was simple, but its roots ran deep – a complete system of conduct, whose foundations the brothers laid down calmly and carefully: "You are a Muslim, and Islam means surrender to God's rule, submission to Him, and belief in the miraculous verses of the Noble Qur'an and in the Hadiths reporting the Prophet's words and deeds." One might say, logically speaking, that they had demolished the old building first and then laid down the foundations of the new, but this analogy would be an overly mechanical depiction of a process of the human soul. It would be more accurate to say that a combination of emotional, logical, and textual currents had swept a number of elements, all of which were stagnant, lifeless, and doomed, out of their path. Faith and unbelief now had, within my heart, far wider meanings than the narrow ones that the society around me had defined for them. These other members of society considered that they could cheat God, fob Him off with a few mumbled phrases, and then improvise how to live a life they hadn't even had a hand in creating. From now on, my understanding of the universe would be formed by God's rules and by the sunna of His Prophet. "*Whoso judges not according to what God has sent down – they are the unbelievers,*" (Qur'an 5:44) would chant the brother who was our preacher. Then, raising his voice, he would continue: "Could anything be clearer? Could anything be more explicit? God Almighty declares, from His abode above the seven heavens, that whoever does not rule according to His shari'a that He revealed is an unbeliever. Then along comes some miserable human, who eats and drinks, and wipes his shit off with his hand, and says, 'No, he's not an unbeliever!'" Following such emotional outbursts, the speaker would go on to set forth first the religious proofs derived from the Qur'an, then the Prophetic Hadiths, and finally the pronouncements of scholars of religion – those scholars of religion, that is to say, who served the truth. Our constitution, the Islamic Action Charter, in a section entitled "Our Understanding," characterized the latter as follows: "We understand Islam, in all its exhaustiveness and inclusiveness, in the same way that the trustworthy scholars of religion of the nation of Islam who follow the sunna of the Prophet Muhammad (pbuh) have understood it."

If a consensus had been achieved among these trustworthy scholars (and not among the scholars belonging to the secular authority, who followed their own whims) then any ensuing fatwa, or decision on a point of religious law, was irrefutable; it was the word of God. And this consensus – and here the brothers would open Ibn Kathir's commentary on the Qur'an so that we could see with our own eyes – exists with regard to the fatwa declaring that the ruler who does not rule according to God's revelation is an unbeliever. We could see the fatwa with our own eyes, and not only that, but in Ibn Kathir's book, which was sold everywhere, was advertised on television, and which people could buy serialized in supplements of the morning newspapers. We learned the fatwa, and we learned another, more important, lesson: that knowledge was a benison that God bestowed on whom He wished, and whom He wished were those sincere believers who had delved into ancient books in order to discover what it was that might restore their nation to that glittering point in its history when "the Islamic state stretched from China in the east to Spain and Portugal in the west," when Harun al-Rashid would look at a cloud passing over his balcony and say to it, "Go thou east or go thou west, the taxes on the yield of thy rain shall come to me," when "each grain of wheat was the size of a date," and when "al-Mu'tasim sent forth an army because a Muslim woman taken captive by the Frankish armies had cried out, 'Woe is Mu'tasim!'"

Perhaps because of his name, I would picture Ibn Kathir (literally, Son of Abundance) in the form of a man flying over a stretch of land, his broad mantle spread out like the wings of some mythical bird. His beard was black mixed with white, even though his face was still that of a young man, and in this flying form he hovered forever, low over a river in Iraq – specifically – holding in his hand a piece of paper resembling an Egyptian papyrus and a quill pen. The words of his book, and those of other ancient books whose language I labored to understand, would take me to a beautiful place that had no resemblance to the time of defeat in which we lived. The difference between the two times was – to use the concept favored by societies that love the past – like that between the art of the good old days and the bad art of today: the first was something people knew from the past and spoke about on television programs and in newspaper articles. Our beautiful time, too, had its cognoscenti. True, they hadn't experienced it first hand, but they traced their origins to it. They resembled it in their characteristics, they resembled it in their way of speaking, and they resembled it in their way of thinking. They came from a time that I did not know and that my friends did not know, and since the equation had only two times and no more, they must certainly have come from that other time – the time of the ancient books, the cloud, the cry to al-Mu'tasim, the giant grain of wheat, and the vast map. Their words were the starting point, after which everything would proceed as God had ordered: *Yet had the people of the cities believed and been god-fearing, we would have opened upon them blessings from heaven and earth* (Qur'an 7:96).

What brought us together with these trustworthy scholars of religion was the divine truth, the dependable rope, the sinew that preserved for the nation's religion its undeviating integrity, and preserved for the word of God its divinity. The preacher would close his five fingers, pressing the tips together as tightly as he could, as though holding a pen, which he would point toward the sky, writing in the air and then reading what he had written: "The divine nature of the source." This – "the divine nature of the source" – was the most important thing that distinguished our way. This was what made us confident that we possessed the truth. "The divine nature of the source" – this was what determined what we believed and held as our creed, far removed from capricious flip-flopping and fanciful conceits: *What is there*, as the Almighty says, *after truth, but error?* (Qur'an 10:32). The truth was one and could not be many, just as the Almighty Truth, glory be to Him, was one and could not be many. Everything other than that, every aberration or lapse or deviation from the Straight Path was a deviation from this truth and from the path of truth: *What is there, after truth, but error?* The Messenger (pbuh) drew a line with his finger, then around that line he drew other lines and recited the words of the Almighty, *"And this is My path, straight; so do you follow it, and do not follow divers paths lest they scatter you from His path"* (Qur'an 6:153). And the Messenger said that his nation

| 48 |

would be scattered into seventy-three branches, all of whom were destined for the Fire, except for one.

All of us knew which one would not enter the Fire – the one that followed the truth, and proclaimed it openly.

The brothers openly proclaimed the truth at the start of the second term of Hosni Mubarak's presidency at the end of 1987, their strength and determination bringing extra confidence to my admiration for them. Who said they were ancient books? In their hands, these books now addressed politics and people's concerns better than the newspapers. Indeed, even in the case of a modern political construct such as the parliamentary elections, the Jama'a went back to those same books, issuing a booklet entitled *Ilah ma'a Allah?* (A God beside God?) endorsing a booklet issued by the Tawaqquf wa-l-Tabyin group entitled *al-Qawl al-sadid fi bayan anna majlis al-sha'b munaf li-l-tawhid* (The Unanswerable Word Explaining How the People's Assembly Is Incompatible with the Oneness of God). The Tawaqquf wa-l-Tabyin group, to which belonged the man who questioned me on the excuse of ignorance, was heretically innovative, and yet, in this work, it had been guided to the truth to which our group had also found its way; thus there was no problem with benefiting from its teachings. The divine truth was one, to those who had eyes.

When I put on one of the oily perfumes that were sold at the doors of mosques, my mother would show her revulsion at the smell and my sister would make fun of it. Still, things would go on as normal and no one would demand that I bathe and get rid of the smell. The tapes of Islamist songs, of which I had by then formed a 'library,' were not to the taste of anyone else at home. As far as my mother was concerned, they were something from an era she did not know, for even though she had put on a headscarf following the birth of my brother, her third child, in 1980, she remained to that point lukewarm toward her religion and didn't pray. She had completed her university studies in 1979 at the age of twenty-eight, so had experienced the period when university girls, even

in Asyut, kept up with the fashion for above-the-knee skirts and
sleeveless blouses. It was she who'd taught me to make the cinema
a part of my life by taking me there as a child. From her, too, I'd
acquired a love of Abd el-Halim Hafez. I was five years old the
day he died. The television interrupted its programming and the
picture of an airplane appeared, followed by the voice of Abd el-
Halim singing, "Farewell, this world of bliss. Farewell, my love and
dreams.... . The lifetime of my wounds is longer than this life."
What I remember though is another song of his, the one that says,
"We set off, but how I fear the end! Heaven or Hell? Ah, what a
choice! I leave but am confused. Ah, how I fear!" In this version
of the memory, I, as a child, ask, "Did Abd el-Halim know he was
going to die?" This version lodged itself more and more firmly
in my memory, especially after I started spending time with the
brothers, because of the lesson in faith that it carried. The answer
to Abd el-Halim's question was obvious: "Hell, of course, and a
terrible fate!" I remember the day of his death because of the one
indisputable thing about it: my mother took off her glasses and
wiped tears from her eyes for 'the Arab Frank Sinatra,' who had
died aged just forty-eight.

My mother never became involved in this new world of mine,
and I never sought to involve her, except in matters where religion intersected with the manly pride of the adolescent that I had
become. Thus I'd get mad if she stood on the balcony in a house-
dress that became see-through in the sunlight or took something
off the washing line without first covering her hair. I did, however,
pay attention to what my sister, who was four years older than I,
thought about the aesthetic side of things. I considered her the
ultimate judge of voices and songs. She'd played the accordion
since she was young and was in the school band and the Asyut
Governorate Music Band. She was convinced that I was incapable
of any vocal activity more complicated than singing to myself in
the bathroom, and that in a low voice. My sister didn't like the
Islamist songs either, and she didn't like the way I recited the
Qur'an. When I asked her to listen to a new tape, she'd sit down
like someone compelled to do so out of politeness. In a word, all
my family agreed that these songs of mine concerned them from

one perspective only, which was that I shouldn't raise the volume of the cassette player high enough for people on the street to hear.

The songs, the vocabulary, the perfumes, the new concerns, and my vision of the world – all these things I regarded as belonging to the same category as a smell that disappears soon after one opens the window, and the fact that my beard had not yet sprouted gave me the feeling that I still had plenty of time. This was confirmed when, a few days before adopting the brothers' famous, short jalla-biya, I was walking in the street and greeting my old friends, most of them Christians, whom I hadn't run into for a while, and they were unaware of any difference, and those who hadn't heard about the change that had occurred in me from the gossip among their fellow students didn't behave differently toward me in any way. Everything was hidden behind a youthful face and modern cloth-ing. Then, however, I decided to reveal these changes to the world, gathering them all into a single symbol. Then, and only then, did I make the commitment. I decided that I would wear a short jal-labiya of the type worn by the brothers. This was a difficult step for me. Everything I'd done up to that point was, like the smell, short-lived, and its relationship to the rest of my life ambiguous. What I was doing now, though, had a color, a color that was more authen-tic and less easily got rid of; it was easier to distinguish and could be seen at a distance. Light blue was my jallabiya, and beneath it I wore white baggy ankle-length drawers. I also bought a white shawl that I wound round my head, and a second, white, jallabiya.

My father was furious at what I'd done. Wearing the jalla-biya was, for me, a response to the evolution of my relationship with the Jama'a and my relationship with my brothers. I wanted to look like them. Some of them had regarded the delay in my adoption of Islamist dress as unjustifiable, and of a piece with my initial finickiness about eating with my hand from the same dish as others. My father himself wore a jallabiya from time to time when he wasn't at work – a jallabiya of a kind in keeping with his village origins. He had lived in Asyut since entering university in 1962, but he continued throughout his life to work in the city of Tema, close to his village, traveling fifty kilometers daily each way. My paternal uncles, and sometimes my mother, used to say that what had happened to me was my father's fault because he would allow me to argue with him about anything – even soccer, where we supported two different teams. My father, who, because of his short temper, was sometimes extremely harsh, permitted us to do things that others would not have. For example, my sister rode a bicycle in the village when she was twelve years old, and got herself followed by crowds calling to one another to come and see this extraordinary event. My father, however, didn't punish her and I don't even remember him rebuking her. Likewise, he didn't do anything to me when he found out that I'd been to see an adults-only movie when I was eleven, apart from extracting a promise from me that I wouldn't do it again. It was the same when he heard that I'd called his sister a bad word (the meaning of which I didn't understand). So why was my father so upset now?

Islamist dress – the Islamist jallabiya – is a Pakistani garment that, while not resembling in every detail the dress that the Prophet wore, reproduces it in general terms in that it is a modest, wide garment that hides the contours of the body. More importantly, it doesn't look like anything worn by non-Muslims. This distinction is – in the eyes of the Jama'a – an indication of their complete disassociation from the acts of those who disobey God and a distinguishing mark that separates them from other Muslims, and non-Muslims. The prophets did the same. Moses (pbuh) received a divine command to distinguish his believing followers from the Egyptians, followers of Pharaoh: *And We revealed to Moses and his brother, "Take you, for your people, in Egypt, certain houses, and make your houses a qibla; and perform the prayer; and do thou give good tidings to the believers"* (Qur'an 10:87), the meaning being, on the authority of Ibn Abbas and Sa'id ibn Jubayr, "And make your houses facing one another." According to the brothers, the objective of God's order to the Jews to set their houses up facing one another was to distinguish them from the houses of those who disobeyed God. His command to this effect, despite His knowledge that this would make it easier for the followers of Pharaoh to identify and seize them, was an indication that some mighty divine wisdom, known only to Him, glory be to Him, pertained to the matter. This wisdom may have consisted in – in addition to distinguishing between them and the unbelievers should God's wrath fall upon the latter – teaching them psychologically that they were different from others, for they were His special people, chosen from among all the rest. Similarly, the introduction of distinctions generates loyalty, mutual love, and respect among the members of a group of humans, the example being (as the brother who was teaching us would tell us) the close bonds that grow up among minorities, or even within any group that comes together over something that its members have in common, such as motorcyclists, the person most concerned to help someone with a broken bike being another motorcyclist. For the same reason, the brothers insisted on letting their beards grow, even though doing so made it easier for the security forces to follow them and in spite of the fact that they viewed the shaving of the beard as permissible, in order to avoid persecution by the enemies of God.

For the uncommitted, this idea was hard to swallow. But it was a fact that food was tastier when we sat down to eat in the same manner, each of us tucking his left foot under his buttocks, while the right formed an inverted 'V,' like the shape of the Arabic numeral eight, and each of us drinking his glass of water in precisely three swallows. The feeling of being a group became even more firmly entrenched when it evolved into a common look that made the members of the group recognizable to one another wherever they might go. They would let their beards grow, ungroomed and uncut, to the breadth of a fist, clip their mustaches so that they wouldn't look like Magians, and not pluck their eyebrows so as not to be mistaken for women. From the pocket of one's jallabiya (which we called a 'shirt') peeked the tip of a miswak, or chewing stick, with which we cleansed our mouths of any remnants of matter; and those same mouths were never used to whistle, as we had to distinguish ourselves from the unbelievers of Mecca, who, before Muhammad's mission, used to whistle as they walked around God's Sacred House – a small thing, but one that helped to deepen our sense of continuity over thousands of years. History, like us, proceeded along tracks that had a defined route and a predetermined end. It, like us, was engaged in an infinitely ancient and eternal struggle between obedience and disobedience, between believers and unbelievers. The Jews, in the days of the pharaohs, and the Christians, up to the time of Muhammad's mission, had been our allies because in those days they had defended the message of God's oneness; now they were our enemies because they had not accepted the message of Islam. Even the history of the Muslims was, for us, the history of their faith, the history of how far their ideas conformed to the pure creed. The sole reason for the departure of the various Islamic sects from the truth was that they were sick in their souls, and had chosen to distinguish themselves from the straight path as followed by the only sect that would be saved. This was a general rule that was to be applied to all, so as to divide the entire world, past and present, into believers and unbelievers. To the first group – such as those fighting jihad in Afghanistan – would go victory, and to the second – such as the Russian unbelievers – would go defeat, for the angels fought in the ranks of the believers. The civil war had broken out in Lebanon because corruption had reached huge proportions there and God had decided to destroy its people: *And when We desire to destroy a city, We command its men who live at ease, and they commit ungodliness therein, then the Word is realized against it, and We destroy it utterly* (Qur'an 17:16). The tornadoes that afflicted the United States were a manifestation of God's wrath, and any earthquake that might strike the earth was a warning from God to people that their time would come soon. Afflictions visited on believers were a test of their faith that would raise them to greater heights, and the failure of rains was a trial imposed by God that could be lifted only through the prayers of righteous men. *Al-Aydz – 'iqab Allah* (AIDS – God's Punishment) says the title of a book published in 1986; on the front cover are flames and on the back the following Hadith of the Prophet: "Never does a people appear openly practicing debauchery but God afflicts them with sicknesses and pains for which there is no cure."

It was the bicycle chain that had drawn me into my new world but once there I found things that suited me better. My slight physique and cowardice in a fight created a distance between me and the possibility of my ever becoming a hero of physical strength, one equal to that between the sun and Mercury, Mercury revolving in the orbit of the light of faith that encompasses all people (Mercury in this case being me). Compared to other children at school, I was advanced in two things – rote memorization and arithmetical calculation. The first of these was, no doubt about it, the route by which I might be able to distinguish myself within the Jama'a. In the first year, I tried weightlifting and learning how to get the flick knife out of my pocket in the open position or to open it against my forehead, which was one of those tricks that dazzled and frightened an opponent. Something in my heart, however, resembled whatever lay in the heart of the Lion in *The Wizard of Oz*, and this was a sickness for which there was no cure. When the Jam'iya Shar'iya was raided, I ran around in a state of panic before reaching the house. I was incapable of standing like the man with the crutch and yelling, "Stand firm: your religion is under attack!" I was incapable too of finding in myself the things that I saw in my daydreams – a strong heart and feet that never retreated. What astonished me, though, when I asked Sheikh Tareq for the first time about a religious ruling, was the readiness with which he answered and his capacity to produce from memory the evidence, in the form of verses from the Qur'an, Prophetic Hadiths, and pronouncements of religious scholars, and then to quote in each case the source from which they were taken. I felt like a dwarf before this amazing torrent of sayings and exemplary deeds. And when I saw Sheikh Umar Abd el-Rahman and heard him preach, I realized that it is the scholars who set the brave on their course, not the reverse, and that it wasn't important to deal blows to be brave; what mattered was to stand firm as Sheikh Umar, who was blind and couldn't see his enemies, much less fight them, had stood firm. One of the older brothers told me that one day Sheikh Umar was on his way to a certain mosque, where he was going to preach. As usual, everything was shrouded in secrecy, but the police found out his plans and set up roadblocks on every street leading to the mosque. The driver of the car in which Sheikh Umar was riding, presented with the sight of rows of soldiers in front of him, panicked and wanted to turn around, and all the brothers in the car panicked too, except for the sheikh. He yelled at the driver to step on the gas pedal and drive right at them, which he did, the throngs of soldiers dividing in confusion and fleeing before the speeding car, which seemed almost to know its way.

The road started with one who knew himself well, including both his strong and weak points. I started by memorizing a small part of the Qur'an and a lot of Hadiths and pronouncements of scholars as well as their fatwas on specific subjects. I discovered that it wasn't as difficult as it had seemed when I had listened to Sheikh Tareq for the first time and that after two months one could become well-versed in religious matters, after the manner of those who solve crossword puzzles, possessing a narrow world of knowledge that they review every day until they are capable of solving the puzzle in five minutes, while others (and only others) are dazzled by what they can do. With the enthusiasm of a learner and the freshness of the facts in my mind, I even started confidently quizzing Sheikh Tareq. There is something irresistibly attractive about this kind of limited knowledge that allows one to memorize a lesson as is, and then show off what one knows in one's discussions with other people, taking on the role of the teacher. My fancy was particularly taken by those books that derive the strategic steps to be taken from religious first principles, so that theory takes on a modern garb and the door is opened for it to go out and take a stroll among the people. I refer, of course, to the books of Sayyid Qutb. I learned parts of these by heart and started imitating his writing style the way other adolescents imitate the poetry of Nizar Qabbani. The brothers awarded me the title of Sayyid Qutb the Younger, and simpler sorts, when they listened to me, began praising me with expressions such as "God grant you victory, my son!" and "The other kids like him smoke and sit around in cafés, while he's a man, and knows Our Lord."

This limited degree of knowledge, which brought with it no responsibilities, consisted of a mixture of innocence, foolishness, and ambition, and the same components were present in that same simple degree of commitment. During the first days, everything was easy and new – more beautiful than the figures and more smoothly moving than the fractions of seconds on the digital watch you'd been given as a child. You'd stop from time to time to make sure that the numbers were real and not an optical illusion. Indeed, the figures did have fractions; they were of very little value but they were there. Your concentration was directed entirely on savoring the thing, whatever it might be, not on delving deeply into it; on attracting it to you, not on pushing it away. Up to that time, I had been happy to grow and get older, racing to an appointment with the little hairs that I was waiting to appear on my face. I don't believe that I have experienced a sensation like it since.

✳

I went to Sheikh Tareq's shop and stayed there the whole day. This was not something I usually did. Several times I evaded the question, "What's wrong with you?" answering, "Nothing. I just want to stay here." I didn't know how to broach the subject with him. A fair time had passed in my life without my talking about personal, intimate matters. I thought I'd put them behind me. I really did hold to my decision not to watch television or listen to songs that "stimulate the appetites." I also fasted every Monday and Thursday. I divided my time between the brothers and school, which had been boys-only since I had entered First Preparatory four years before. I'd even abandoned boyish fooling around, with its sexual undertones, whether in the form of jokes, or of our hitting one another on our privates, or of ogling women teachers over or under the school desks. For novels I'd substituted religious books, and for pictures of naked women loaded inside pens with magnifying glasses in their ends I'd substituted watching films about jihad. I was supposed to be a person of unbearable spiritual lightness, whose back would soon take on a permanent curvature from stooping over books and keeping my eyes on the ground out of modesty as I walked the streets. How, then, was I to explain to him what had happened?

The road in front of Sheikh Tareq's store leads directly to the entrance to the University of Asyut. Boys and girls coming from the university pass that way in their hundreds. All the Secondary school girls who go down the same road wear a dark blue uniform with a white shirt. University girls are something else: some of them come from the governorates of conservative Upper Egypt, and some from the governorates of the north. The latter are more liberated in their dress, and some wear see-through shirts and tight jeans. I did not look at these, however, since I was sitting with Sheikh Tareq and wearing Islamist dress for all to see, not to mention that they were at least two years older than me and their clothes made them look much older than that. Were these really the reasons that made me avoid looking at them, or did I fear God? "The glance is an arrow of Satan's. Whoever guards against it out of fear of God, God will grant him in its place a faith whose sweetness he will find in his heart," as the Sinless One (pbuh) said.

It was, however, another matter that had brought me here, something much more important than a mere look, whether a first or a second.

Sheikh Tareq was a humane interlocutor blessed with an innate gift. You felt drawn to talk to him by the fact that he would talk about himself, not with regard to the same subject, but about other subjects. What I had felt and what I had done were far nastier than anything Sheikh Tareq might do, or even think of doing. He told me about his upbringing in his hometown, the village of Musha, from which Sayyid Qutb, no less, hailed. He talked to me about his brother, who had been arrested too but who had shaved off his beard after leaving prison, got married, and devoted himself to his family. He spoke to me for the first time of the operation he had had on his heart and how he had to be careful not to do too much so as not to overwork his cardiac valves. He would, however, be able to get married; this the doctors had confirmed. When I was a little younger, my sister had tricked me one evening into thinking that she had heart disease but didn't want to tell our father and mother so that they wouldn't be sad. That night I took upon myself their entire burden of sorrow and couldn't stop crying. I determined to tell my parents in the morning so that they could do whatever might be in their power. I was afraid that my sister would end up like Soad Hosni in that movie where she dies after going for a swim because she has a weak heart. In the morning, however, I discovered that the whole thing was no more than a silly joke. The disease that Sheikh Tareq confided in me about was neither imaginary nor a joke. We were believers and spoke only the truth, even when making merry. We might report the time off by a minute or two just to make things easier but we did so only after having received a fatwa saying that this was permissible; had we not done so, the child's watch with its fractions of seconds would have proved a difficult challenge. Likewise, according to the fatwa, we could lie to the security forces. In all other matters, we were to speak only the truth, and that was what I did.

A girl who was a friend of the family had spent a whole day at our house when I was there. This had happened just the day before. I stayed for as long as she was present, and all the while that she was looking at my books on the bookshelf and asking me about them, I was resisting the idea of hugging her to me from behind. I'd go up close to her, then retreat and hover about her. I'd approach once again till I was right behind her; she'd give no sign that she was aware that I was there, and I'd move away again. Then I started going close to her and pretending to strangle her, saying, "Why don't you wear a headscarf? You're grown up now." I'd pretend to strangle her but I was enjoying the feel of her body and wanted to pull her toward me. I had never experienced these feelings before. The last time I'd kissed a girl, I'd been seven. We were playing doctors. I'd asked her mother to make cocoa for us. Then I made her lie on the bed and lay on top of her, as I'd seen in the movies. For eight years, I hadn't been close to a girl, and that hadn't mattered to me. Dribbling the soccer ball between my feet and throwing myself on top of it when I was goalkeeper were my greatest pleasures. Girls, as vague images and pictures and conversations among boys, came far behind. Now, in the presence of one of them, when I got close to her, my body changed in ways that made me realize that the last time had indeed been child's play, and what had happened before had been meaningless. The parts of her that I looked at and my sense of what I wanted to do with her were totally different.

"I never thought, Sheikh Tareq, that fornication was something that I would have to struggle against one day. I believed that the major sins only occurred to depraved and evil people, and that our infractions were just the little ones that one could be absolved of from one prayer to the next, from one Friday to the next, from one Ramadan to the next, a belief that reassured my heart that I would reach the Day of Judgment pure and chaste. Today, however, I don't want to go home because she will be there too and I don't want to be put in that position again."

Sheikh Tareq thought that I had behaved well. He praised me and repeated the Hadith of the Prophet, "Be on your guard against the world, and be on your guard against women, for the first strife among the Children of Israel was over women."

I went up to my usual daily place, one of the students' rooms on the roof of our house, at the back. The window of the room looked out onto the rear windows of a building not more than five meters from ours. I'm not good at estimating distances, so it may have been less than that; I'd sometimes thought of using a long stick to pull one of the windows on the floor opposite open a few centimeters, and the stick couldn't have been five meters in length, so it must have been less. The shutter would have been closed or opened enough to leave a small space between its two leaves; I don't want to get into the game of estimating distances again, so let's say ten centimeters, approximately the length of the metal fastener that holds the two wooden leaves fast shut if we want to close the shutters completely. Every day, at a quarter to six in the evening, a girl would come. If the shutters were closed, she'd open them a little, and if they were open, she'd close them partially, in either case securing them with the metal fastener. It was a small space, but I'd become addicted to looking through it and I couldn't imagine that I wouldn't do so that day, whatever the consequences. But that day the room was padlocked.

Sex had not been absent in the days of my religious commitment preceding puberty, but had been an extension of play. Before one of the study circles, Walid informed us that the brothers had a list of books that one had to have permission to read, and this was given only to those preparing for marriage. He mentioned *Tuhfat al-'arus* (The Bride's Treasure) and *Kayf tus'id al-mar'a zawjaha* (How a Woman Can Make Her Husband Happy). Three of us had actually read them, and I bought copies at the earliest opportunity. They contained anecdotes about intercourse and advice to the Muslim wife about how to make her husband reach the heights of pleasure without violating the rules of the Book and the Sunna. The best thing about them, though, was the stories about the great coquettes of Islamic history. Among these was one who was celebrated for the sounds that she made during intercourse. There was also a story about one who couldn't sleep one night because something was pricking her delicate form. The master of the house ordered that the bed be searched time and time again to discover the cause, which turned out to be just a hair, which all the layers of bedding could not prevent her delicate body from feeling. Entertaining stories similar to those of *The Thousand and One Nights*.

With the onset of puberty, however, the desire for sex becomes something entirely different, a hungry beast that knows by instinct what it has to do. I picked up a thick stick that I found discarded in a corner of the roof and inserted it behind the metal tongue in the wall that was connected to the place where the padlock was on the door, then pushed it upward with all my strength until I wrenched the tongue completely off and opened the door to the room. I was not surprised to find in it the belongings of a new tenant, this being the only explanation for the presence of the padlock. I didn't worry about what might happen, or how I was to return things to their former state. Fixing the tongue back on the wall didn't need more than a couple of screws, and the two I'd pulled out would do the trick. All I could think about was what I'd seen the day before and the days before that. This wasn't my only observation post. I'd stand behind the closed shutters at home to look at the legs of our neighbor in the opposite house, from whose face I'd avert my gaze if I saw her on the street. Once I stood there for three straight hours without realizing. From the apartment in which my uncles who were students lived, I'd watch another neighbor woman who would change her clothes in a room with the light on and with the window covered only by a white, semi-transparent curtain. It was because of her that I came to love slim bodies with large breasts that looked like hers, in a black slip and brassiere. I hadn't yet seen anything like that from the room on the roof, which was precisely what made me so persistent. All I would see was a woman's body entering and leaving the room, and sometimes I would see two feet and a part of the legs stretched out on the bed, the rest of which was hidden by the wall. I sensed that many things must happen behind that wall, which, if the windows had been exactly opposite one another, I might have been able to see. The girl in the room received visits from her girl friends late in the evening. For years I'd wanted to see two women together. A friend of mine at the faculty housing told me when we were in First Preparatory that he'd seen his neighbor take off all her clothes in front of her girl friend and my uncle on my father's side had told me that he'd seen two women together from the roof of one of the houses in the village; one of them had twisted the end of her jallabiya to make a penis and then inserted it into the other woman's vagina. I had a strong sense that from this room I'd see something totally new, and that I was going to see it that day.

Despite all of which, I did not like my standing behind the shutters. I knew it was forbidden by religion and I begged God's forgiveness frequently. Imam al-Shafi'i saw the heel of a woman over whom he had no conjugal rights and became incapable of learning the lesson he was studying. Previously, he'd been accustomed to hide the page of the book opposite the one he was reading because his memory would absorb everything he saw instantaneously. He made up the following verse about the incident:

I complained to a trusty man of my poor memory.
"Leave all sin," was his advice.
"Know that knowledge is light," said he,
"And God's light will ne'er shine on one immured in vice."

I would console myself that what I was doing was not one of the seven deadly sins and therefore could be disavowed when I performed my next daily, or Friday prayer, or fasted the coming

Ramadan, and that I would repent, as I would of another thing I'd become addicted to since I'd reached puberty a little while previously, and somewhat late, after the age of fifteen. Friends had told me, as I was anxious, that I was lucky that my sexual maturity was late in coming, because the latter imposed on one certain consequences and religious duties, the least of which was having to perform a complete ritual ablution before setting off to say the dawn prayer if one woke up having experienced a nocturnal emission; this was particularly hard in the cold of winter. They were right. Performing ablutions before the dawn prayer was a problem to which I could find no solution other than masturbating the night before, then washing, and then going to sleep, in which case I would not have any wet dreams. This, however, turned into a custom that I hated even more than playing peeping tom. The fluid would stay in my underwear and I'd smell its piercing aroma and feel that those round me could smell it too. I didn't masturbate in the room on the roof because I went there at an unsuitable time, before my sunset and evening prayers. In my own room, things were different, and the timing was later in the evening. I would masturbate without using my right hand, then go to the bathroom at the time that suited me and deluge my body with water in such a way that it reached every part of it, as prescribed in the Sunna. I would wash in a certain order – my right side before my left, the front before the back, the upper part before the lower.

I didn't touch any of the new tenant's belongings. My eyes were trained on the window, my ears alert to any sound from the stairs, as I was expecting the resident of the room to turn up at any moment. I hoped that what I saw from the window would be worth all the trouble. To tell the truth, this wasn't the first time I'd found myself in difficulties because of my roof adventures. A month earlier, the people in the next building had sensed the presence of someone there and one of them had gone to my father to tell him, in case it was a thief. When my father came up, I told him I was just "getting some fresh air." Another time, my arm unintentionally knocked against a loose brick. It fell, and I heard a scream of terror from the tenant on the ground floor. I immediately fled back to our apartment. I had a simple plan of escape should I hear the footsteps of the new tenant in time, which was not guaranteed. On this occasion, and against normal practice, by the time it was almost seven o'clock, no one had come to the room opposite. This had happened before, but under different circumstances. This time I wouldn't be able to stay there as long as I wanted, as I had done before. I left the room as it was and departed, as though I'd had no hand in the damage that had been done, and it was in this state that I heard about the room that had been broken into and from which nothing had been taken.

All the same, I was aware of danger. How long would God go on protecting me and not expose me? I would make an oath to God, out loud, day after day, the moment I woke up, that I would never play the peeping tom again and that I wouldn't practice "the secret vice" that day; and the day's plan would work. Sometimes a desire to masturbate would come to me early in the day and I would do so, and then make a new oath for the rest of the day. Just once, I broke my oath and I fasted for three days. Then I stopped making the oath, out of fear that it might be considered mockery of God and tried to force myself by willpower. Sometimes I would succeed and sometimes I would fail. The number of women swelled. There were the women on the road in front of Sheikh Tareq's store. There were the scantily clad women on the television screen. I would hear the sound of the squabble between the legs of the sisters in the Jama'a and their modest dresses. I would think of their desires for marriage and bearing children. The sight of girls clutching books to their bosoms on their way home from school or university would excite me. And books would excite me. There were the novels that I had moved from our apartment to a room in the basement, especially Alberto Moravia's *Disobedience*, in a poor translation – these I brought back, along with other novels, and kept on my bookshelf, hiding them behind the books on religion. All I retained of them were the hot scenes. My cousin told me that in one of the novels of his *Trilogy*, Naguib Mahfouz makes a character say of a woman sitting in a horse-drawn cab that her backside was like a dome, and that beneath every dome there lay a sheikh, and he was the sheikh, so I went searching through the entire three novels looking for the sentence. My deeds were further proof that this society was obdurately sinful and completely sunken in filth, and that the solution was to speed up the establishment of the State of the Divine Man, which would help its citizens to be obedient to God. Islam has taught us that female finery and the uncovering of a woman's face are the source of lust. Marriage, on the other hand, without onerous conditions and at a young age, and the concubines that used to be given to a young man when he reached puberty, were the legitimate outlets that men cannot do without. In the Dissolute State, on the other hand, the stimuli of lust were on the increase and its legitimate outlets on the decline.

I locked myself in my room and hung a piece of paper on the door on which was written in large letters the words that Shakespeare, some of whose works I had read in simplified translations, had put in the mouth of Hamlet: "If the old man drowns in the sea of lust, what value can virtue have in the eyes of the young?"

My mother couldn't understand what had taken possession of me. She sent a letter to the amir of the Jama'a, Ahmad Abduh, complaining about my change of attitude. He suggested to me that I see a psychologist who was a member of the Jama'a and who could talk to me about the causes of my behavior. I don't know why, in another of those spasms of irresponsibility that I seemed incapable of getting through my life without, I was delighted. I went back to him later and asked him, in high spirits, when I was going to see the doctor. He looked at me without interest and said, "You don't need a doctor and 'you're not possessed by an afreet,'" meaning that there was nothing whatsoever wrong with me. Talking of afreets, a brother who was with me at school told me that our friend Muhammad, also a committed brother, had started seeing a female genie, who came to him at night and slept with him and treated him just like a husband. He also said that she came to him each night in a different shape and that Muhammad had told him that she was as beautiful as any human woman but with one difference: she would change the form of the beauty every time and was able to come to him at any time without anyone seeing her. Muhammad told the brothers about her and they decided to bring in a brother from Minya to cast her out. I was too scared to attend this exercise in spiritualism but our mutual friend told me afterward, in terror, that Muhammad had spoken to the exorcist in a woman's voice, and that he had clapped his hands and sung in her silky tones, "I love Muhammad and he loves me. I love Muhammad and he loves me." The genie had told them that she was sixty-four years old, and had given the precise number of police cars parked in front of the Jam'iya Shar'iya mosque and a precise description of the members of the security forces who were there, even though they were at least two kilometers away. My friend had gone himself, he told me, and confirmed the accuracy of her descriptions.

I envied Muhammad this daily visit from the genie that loved him. I wanted to be in his place. I would think about her a great deal before going to sleep, in the belief that thinking about afreets could summon them up. It didn't work, however, and the actual methods used for conjuring up afreets, such as reading the Qur'an backward or urinating on it, were unacceptable to a believer. I just used this female afreet, with whom I had no communication, as material for my fantasies.

Sin did not, however, prevent me from pursuing my program of reading and memorization. By the end of the summer vacation, I had memorized three sections of the Qur'an and a large number of Hadiths, and read quite a few books. At the end of the summer, the brothers tested us on what we'd got out of the lessons and I got the best score. Then the brothers asked the Secondary school students who were members of the Jama'a to write down what they envisaged as the ideal methods for effective Islamist action in their schools throughout the governorate of Asyut. One of the brothers met with us, read out some of the suggestions we'd made, and discussed them. He explained his vision for the development of Islamist action in the Secondary schools that the Jama'a had decided to adopt, and his vision of the organizational hierarchy, when we should meet, and the goals for which we should be held accountable. Also, one of the Brothers of '81 – the term used for the brothers who had gone to prison in 1981 in the aftermath of the killing of Sadat – was chosen to be the ultimate authority responsible for Islamic action in the Secondary schools. The meeting ended with the announcement of the name of the brother who was to be amir of the Secondary School Brothers in Asyut, and it was me. "This means that I can't go on being the way I am" was the first thing to occur to me. It would be my duty as a leader to do my utmost to do better in terms of obedience to God, so that those with me shouldn't be punished by God for my errors. I would never be victorious in any battle if I didn't first conquer my main enemy, my body. I spent more time in prayer each night, I started taking greater care to perform the dawn prayer in the mosque, I fasted five days a week, and I started wearing two types of underwear at the same time – boxers and, over them, a slip, so that I wouldn't have erections. This also provided another advantage – that the area of my private parts wouldn't show through my pants. For the same reason, I stopped wearing jeans or any type of tight pants at all and started wearing my long shirts outside my pants, thus also covering the area below that of my private parts. I wished to appear openly, and conduct myself inwardly, like the leaders of the Jama'a. I even gave up playing soccer. I wanted more time in order to acquire the religious knowledge that I needed in debate, and I wanted more time to come up with methods of proselytization inside the schools.

*

We called the school principal the Tyrant. He was a tough man who dealt resolutely with students of an age at which they are difficult to control. He was never absent for a single day. Looking at us from behind his dark glasses, which people said had been given him by the intelligence services, he would notice the slightest snigger in the back rows and any variation, no matter how small, from the school's blue and gray uniform, even if he were standing on the podium that dominated the school yard. In addition to the dark glasses, he had a cane, which always preceded him by a pace. We ascribed to him the same qualities we did to our ruler. Our school – the Nasser Military Secondary School – was, for us, a miniature version of the military rule under which we lived, and we existed in the hope that he would absent himself from the school for even just one day, so that we could live under a different dispensation. This did indeed happen just before New Year 1988, and we were to pay a high price, even though the whole thing was no more than a joke and not to be compared in any way with other things we had been doing since the beginning of the school year.

I started work in my new role with an unforgivable mistake. I prepared a paper that included a census, with all the names, of the members of the Jama'a in the main schools in which we were going to be active, and the roles that I thought appropriate for them. I gave a copy of this to the Chain Boy whom I considered, given our friendship, my right hand man. Brother Tareq A., however, found the paper discarded in the mosque. He reproached me vehemently, accusing me of negligence, incompetence, and being unequal to the responsibility. Because of pieces of paper such as this, underground groups that the brothers had spent years preparing had been aborted, not to mention the human losses. I was punished with a fine of twenty pounds pending the carrying out of a secondary investigation of myself and the Chain Boy. The latter was fined the same amount; he also received twenty blows to the soles of his feet, however, so that he'd never forget his mistake.

At the beginning of the year, we distributed booklets entitled *Man nahnu wa-madha nurid?* (Who Are We and What Do We Want?) to introduce the Jama'a to the students. These were written in simple language and answered basic questions that tended to arise concerning Islamist action. We had been taught in our lessons on methods of proselytization that there was always common ground to be found between us and any individual. These were the broad issues dealing with the dignity and self-respect of the Islamic nation, confronting aggression and plots, and ridding ourselves of corruption and corrupt persons. We had two breaks during the school day, a short one of a quarter of an hour, and a long one of an hour that was devoted to extracurricular activities. A week after the start of the school year, the school canceled the soccer league, as usual; there was a large number of students and effort was needed to keep them under control, while the teachers thought that this activity was a waste of the students' and their own time. We started forming study circles during this break. We would recite Qur'an, or one of the brothers would prepare a lesson and deliver it, or we'd exchange ideas on some topic. Sometimes we'd sing. The school's response to the circles we organized was to organize their own religious study groups, led by the Sufi teacher who spoke of "grace," and "miraculous powers," and "mystic intuition." We'd raise questions with him about the judgment of religion on singing, or on looking at women outside the family, and whether one who ruled according to anything other than God's revelation was an unbeliever, and was interest on bank accounts a form of usury. And when the school closed the doors of the mosque for the afternoon prayer, on the grounds that this prayer time fell at the end of the school day and that our call to prayer delayed the closing of the school doors, our response was to hold the prayer collectively in the yard every day, and we went on doing this until the principal himself forbade us to do so any longer.

On the day in question, however, the tyrannical principal was absent, and it was our duty to exploit the situation.

We had to find an issue around which we could rally a large number of the students, and it wasn't easy. Those who sympathized with us were many but an issue that united them all was hard to find, and harder still was the issue about which we could imagine some simple oppositional act, something that was easy and brief. We found our issue by pure coincidence – the morning assembly salute to the flag with the cheer "Long Live the Arab Republic of Egypt!" (to be repeated three times in a loud voice booming with enthusiasm). To us in the Jama'a, this cheer constituted the sanctification of something other than God, who alone was fit to be regarded as holy. There was to be no nationalism in Islam other than in the sense of the defense of the lands of Islam – defense of Islam in one's home country, not defense of the home country. The brothers would tell us that when the eyes of the Prophet had filled with tears on being expelled by the unbelievers from Mecca, he had said, "By God, you are verily the land of God most beloved to my heart and had not your people expelled me, I would not have left" (Hadith), he was not weeping for his country but for the country that was the most beloved of lands to God. It was the most beloved of lands to God and thus the most beloved to the heart of the Prophet and to the heart of every Muslim in the world because it was the first land of Islam and the home of God's Holy House.

As far as the students were concerned, the flag issue was something we'd sold to them as a joke to celebrate the absence of 'the ruler of the school.' The military officer who led the salute to the flag each day stood up and watched the flag as it was being raised. Then he yelled, as he always did, "Long Live the Arab Republic of Egypt!" only to find thousands responding behind him, "There is no god but God!" The officer himself laughed as he repeated the salute, and the words "There is no go but God" grew louder and louder. We considered it a victory, a tale to be told in a sound bite to those who came after us.

It seems that various officials here and there heard about what had happened in the school, and the administration – in keeping with the policy of the state at the time – started holding seminars in the large hall to explain "true Islam." The speakers on the podium in these seminars were an assortment that included a member of the school board and a member of the ruling National Party, plus a sheikh from al-Azhar. What was said, however, was always the same and concerned the efforts exerted by the government (led by His Excellency the President) to improve the quality of services and freedoms as a way to preserve Islam and spread its call yet wider, and the not less than ninety-nine percent consistency of Egyptian law with the Islamic shari'a. These sessions were of course boring and the arguments weak, and we were, as usual, ready with the questions and the old books that conveyed the consensus of the scholars of religion as to the correctness of the fatwas that we followed.

The laws of society do not vary greatly from the laws of physics that we studied at school. When two forces work in different directions, the result of their action is a force working in an intermediate direction. This was what happened with us and with our society. We were a fundamentalist force convinced of its fundamentalism, and they were a secular force unconvinced of its secularism. We exerted pressure so they exerted pressure and the outcome was that they arrived at a midpoint between the two forces, an area

they believed proved that they had adopted a middle-of-the-
road Islam, as represented by sheikhs whose point of reference
was also Islam, which was our territory, our playing field, and our
banner. This acknowledgment that Islam was the point of reference was in itself a victory for us, though not a sufficient one. We,
as fundamentalists, began from the same original point that we
were at, while leaving them to begin from their new midpoint.
The midpoint then would be closer to our position, and so on
and so forth. A slow change, but real. In the last such session, the
Azhari sheikh became exasperated when we quoted at him what
the "trustworthy" scholars say about the ruler who does not rule
according to God's revelation, or abolishes even one of the punishments specified in the Qur'an, and about the Muslim's obligation
to "command good and forbid evil" in every aspect of our daily
lives. A man of his type was unable to say that the rules of Islam
were cultural norms pertaining to a certain stage, or that we could
look at them from a historical or critical standpoint. Religion was
the sheikh's stock in trade and the source of his livelihood, but the
livelihood came from the job and the job was by gift of the government, or more specifically of the security apparatus. All our poor
sheikh could do was to lose his temper with us while the students
laughed at him. We left the hall and it emptied. The fact is, we and
our sympathizers made up the majority of the audience.

We were now equipped to assert our moral authority, and we
didn't let an opportunity escape us. It came to our ears that on the
Prophet's birthday a Christian student had made a drawing of a
store selling the special candy made for that day and labeled it The
Worm-eaten Candy Store. Some of the brothers waited for him as
he left the school and beat him up, telling him not to try making
fun of Muslims again. Word also got around that one of the students was a sexual 'deviant' and that he was pushing pictures of
abominations among the students, so some brothers from outside
the school went to him and beat him severely, shouting "God is
great! God is great!" as they did so.

My academic level that year wasn't Good, but it was acceptable. No one pays any attention to the second year at Secondary
school, preferring instead to save their effort for the third year,

which determines which university one enters. I was much better at extracurricular activities. I joined the team that represented my school in the school journalism competition and the Arabic Language teacher set me the task of writing a summary of a book by Mustafa Mahmud to represent the school in the governorate's school literary competition. I looked forward to the games period every Wednesday. It was an opportunity to play soccer, and also sometimes to do some gymnastic exercises, of which I particularly liked the run and half-somersault without hands. I was fifteen years and eight months old and I felt fifteen years and eight months old. Those extra months have a special significance in Egypt, where you get an identity card when you reach sixteen, and if a police officer says, "Where's your I.D., boy?" you have to show it. At the age I was then, though, you'd tell him your exact age so that he'd know that you weren't required to carry I.D. February 17, 1988 was a Wednesday. I did my favorite somersault wrong and hurt my back. I could barely walk and a friend undertook to take my bike back home. At the end of that day, however, our school looked like a fortress under siege, with three large Central Security trucks and three armored cars parked outside. What would happen if I was obliged to make a run for it on foot? When it was time for the students to leave, the troops drew themselves up in rows on either side of the gate, holding their shields and with their sticks raised in the air. It was said that they had a list of names and that they had stopped students to ask them their names but hadn't arrested anyone. I left in the middle of the crowd and no one stopped me, so I decided that the intention must be simply to cow us. We were still just adolescents, and green.

The next day I was out of school because of the pain in my back. A school friend phoned me to let me know that the security service had transferred me and five other students from the school to other schools, all of them outside the city of Asyut. The school that fell to my lot was that of Dayrut, sixty-four kilometers to the north. Even when I heard of the decision, I considered it to be no more than a scare tactic. Only a few days before, the governor of Asyut, Muhammad Abd el-Halim Musa, had visited us at the school journalism competition. He shook hands with our group one by one and congratulated us on our exhibit, which was a kind of plaque showing the al-Aqsa Mosque surrounded by a chain with a padlock in the shape of a Star of David.

The following day, my father visited the school and got a taste of how serious the matter was. My parents phoned my uncle on my mother's side, the officer, and he informed them that from his contacts with his friends in State Security things did not bode well. My father didn't lose hope. He contacted acquaintances and local politicians, who promised him they'd solve the problem. I was confident that it would be solved; it was just a matter of time. However, my father's acquaintances withdrew their promises, informing him that the decision came from the upper echelons and no one could interfere with it. So serious was the matter, in fact, that a rumor went round among the students, just to make things even scarier, that Hosni Mubarak had himself phoned the governor, reprimanded him for what was happening at the school, and instructed him to intervene resolutely.

Throughout this period, my parents treated me with controlled reproach. My father rejected the idea of retaining a lawyer from the Jama'a to bring a case against the school because he didn't want things to escalate. I didn't become aware of the strength of the pressures on them, however, until I woke one night to the sound of my sister crying loudly, while my father repeated, "I'll phone for a doctor. I'll phone for a doctor." I entered the room he'd just left, to find my mother stretched out on the bed, her face drawn and her left arm incapable of movement, while my sister sat on the floor, by the bed, holding her hand. My brother, who was then eight, lay on his stomach, hiding his face between his hands without uttering a word, an image that will remain indelibly etched on my memory. I was afraid for my mother and felt a disaster was about to occur. Was it in a situation such as this that the Companion of the Prophet Mus'ab ibn Umayr had said, "Mother, should you have seventy lives and should you depart each life one after the other, I would not abandon this matter"?

How serious things really were came home to me one evening when we were sitting listening to my father as he told us of his trip to see State Security. The officer had kept him waiting three hours before deigning to see him. My father said this, and then broke into tears. I thought of the Prophet's prayer, "O God, I seek refuge with Thee from worry and sorrow, and I seek refuge with Thee from impotence and sloth, and I seek refuge with Thee from subjection to debt and the oppression of men" (Hadith). This was the first visual image of the "oppression of men" that I had earlier learned by heart as part of the Prophet's prayer. It would not be the last.

Two weeks with all their comings and goings passed and I was obliged to go to my new school. During those two weeks, the brothers put on a mass rally in support of the Secondary School Brothers, during which, naturally, our names and the details of what had happened to us were read out. The first time I made a quick visit to the Jam'iya Shar'iya mosque (which for a time my parents forbade me to go to), I met Brother Mahmud Shu'eib, who introduced me to another brother who was standing at his side, pointing me out as one of those transferred from their school. The brother clung to my hand as he shook it, looking me in the eye and then shaking his head while Sheikh Mahmud laid his hand on my shoulder. "I ask you now," said Mahmud. "A regime that would do that to Secondary students, is it not a regime of unbelievers?" and I felt the enormity of what the regime had done, and the hugeness of the sacrifice that I was making. Thereafter brothers would stop me and ask, "Aren't you so-and-so?" and when I answered in the affirmative, the same clinging handshake would be repeated, followed by expressions designed to strengthen the patient in the endurance of tribulation.

I was forbidden to go to the Jam'iya Shar'iya mosque and my father bought me two jallabiyas of traditional cut of the sort he wore himself. One was blue, the other grayish green. I didn't find them suitable but put the blue one on anyway and went to perform the afternoon prayer. On the way, I found myself face to face with a German Shepherd (the breed of dog used by the police), which approached with a slowness that did not inspire confidence. I froze for a moment, then set off at top speed with the dog on my heels. With its wide cut in the lower half and its heavy cloth, the jallabiya was an encumbrance, especially given that it was still new. The sound of its flapping as I ran filled my ears. The thin white jallabiyas that the brothers wear in no way impede movement. What saved me in the end was that the owner of the dog called to it. My brother and sister made fun of me when I told them what had happened and I'm sure the people in the street had laughed at me. I never wore either of those jallabiyas again.

The first day, I went to Dayrut by train and came back by train. The train was cheap and the cost of a ticket was within the limits of my daily allowance. It stopped at all the stations and was intolerably crowded as a result. That was the first and last time. I asked my parents to let me go on the air-conditioned bus that departed at set times and they agreed. The principal of the new school took the same bus daily and this could have become a factor in a good relationship with him. My father gave me a pound and a quarter for transportation evening by evening, maybe because he still had hope that the whole thing would end unexpectedly, or maybe to remind me on a daily basis that my family had to bear their part of the results of my actions.

I would start my day at four-thirty in the morning, pray the dawn prayer in the mosque, and from there go directly on to the bus station. Sometimes I would sit next to the principal and we would talk and sometimes he'd take a later bus and I'd only encounter him on the return journey. The two trips consumed two hours every day not counting the waiting time. Usually on the return journey I slept, resting my head on the glass and not waking until we reached Asyut. Husam, a fellow student who had been transferred with me to Dayrut, usually woke me up. Once a man I didn't know woke me up and pointed out that my saliva had been running down my chin as I slept. I didn't have a Kleenex on me, so he asked another passenger for one. I was so embarrassed I wanted to die.

I wouldn't go to school if I woke up late, I wouldn't go if I dawdled and missed the bus, and I wouldn't go if I was tired out. Eventually my absence days reached twenty-eight and there were only two left before I would be barred from taking the exams. I had only one option left. I stayed away from school for a week, and then went back with a private doctor's certificate stating that I'd been sick. The certificate was a mere formality and it had become customary for any medical certificate to be accepted, because the illness, once passed, was already cured. The principal, however, who imagined himself to be a model civil servant, refused to accept the certificate of his bus companion who'd been transferred to his school as punishment and insisted on my going to the public hospital to have tests before he would sign off on it. The hospital worker gave me a cup in which to put my specimen. I entered the bathroom, positioned the narrow mouth of the cup under my anus, and did what I had been told. I gave the worker the cup and he raised it to take a look, a glass test tube in his other hand. At the point when the hand holding the cup reached the halfway point between his eye and his other hand, he quickly put it back again and looked at it closely. "Yuck! How disgusting! What's this you've gone and done?" he asked me. "It's the specimen," I responded with the utmost simplicity. "The cup's for urine, not shit!" yelled the worker. The other waiting patients exploded in laughter and the disgusted worker transferred the solid matter from the metal cup to a round metal vessel and wrote down for me on a piece of paper the name of the test I was supposed to have performed. There was no mention of the result of the analysis. The finicky principal, however, accepted the paper, convinced that this was confirmation of the accuracy of the medical certificate. The next time, though, the bastard got me. I arrived at school a quarter of an hour late. I was certain I'd be allowed to enter because everyone knew the problems with the transport system between Asyut and there. He did not, however, let me in and I left the school crying like a child, thinking this an injustice that went beyond all bounds of decency, and that God for sure would send him an angel to strike the school with its wings and leave it *a level hollow* (Qur'an 20:106). That day, I returned home convinced that I had carried out my obligations to struggle and be patient to the full, and after weeping, I felt repose in my heart, and faith and confidence, and a resignation to God's decree that was easeful and brought with it peace of mind.

Only a few days later (the transfer was for a total of forty-five days), God's relief arrived. The school board decided to send me back to Asyut, to Marshal Ahmad Isma'il Secondary. True, it wasn't my original school but it would at least relieve me of the inconvenience of the daily journey, and the Chain Boy and other brothers whom I knew were there. I took the end of year exam and just managed to pass, with the lowest score I ever had during my educational career – 57 percent.

Sheikh Tareq looked at Rabso's copybook and found the star, which Rabso's teacher had put on it in kindergarten, unacceptable. Rabso – so called, in reference to the detergent of that name, because he had such shining white skin – was still a child, four years old perhaps. He was proud of the star and loved it, and he was set to grow up loving stars and associating them with superiority and achievement. This was no coincidence, Sheikh Tareq asserted, for the star was the symbol of the Jews.

We were sitting in the Rahma Mosque, to which Rabso's older brother, who was seven, had brought him. Also with us was a university student who wasn't a committed brother but came to the mosque from time to time to chat with us. I made no comment even though the student didn't like what Sheikh Tareq had said. After all, he suggested, it was unreasonable to suppose that the teacher working at the KG was an instrument of World Zionism. Sheikh Tareq did not in fact mean that. He said that the teacher was unaware of the star's meaning, but that the first person to use the star as a symbol of superiority did so for a reason. After a long discussion, the university student said, "Maybe," though he didn't seem convinced. Nor was I, but I hid my doubts behind silence.

In the summer vacation, I resumed my regular contacts with the brothers, once the impact of the events of the school year on my family had abated somewhat. I was convinced that I was a member of that group whether I wanted to be or not, and that nothing would change that fact. I committed one third of the Qur'an to memory, and also went on my first mission to put a stop to an "outrage to religion." On the latter, the Chain Boy and another brother took me to a place, close to the railroad station, where they'd discovered that foreigners bought liquor. When we arrived, the Chain Boy excused himself, on the grounds that he was too fat to be able to run away. Then the other one, who had put us up to the mission in the first place, said that he worked in Old Asyut where there were lots of tourists, and one of them might recognize him. I was the only one left. I picked up two of the stones that made the infill for the railroad tracks and approached the man we'd picked out. He was buying fruit and holding a bag in his right hand. I came up to him from that side, while he was busy talking to the fruit seller. I bent down over the bag and struck the bottle that was inside it with both stones, so that it shattered. Then I set off at a run toward the tracks and kept on running along them. When we got back to the mosque, the brother in charge reproached us because we'd acted without getting permission beforehand. I had known that he'd do so but had gone along with the other two all the same, or at least hadn't opposed them. It was something I did for myself more than for the Jama'a, something like those last few steps that you force yourself to take at the end of a long run. I intended to take a break, to take a longer while off than usual, so I had to do something extraordinary, to remember and be remembered by.

I wasn't preoccupied by the star and Sheikh Tareq's views on it. These were details. I was preoccupied with my performance at school. My educational future would be determined by the marks I made in the Secondary General exam. There was much debate among the brothers over the importance of education, both religious and mainstream. What was certain was that the only mandatory education was that which guaranteed proper performance of one's religion; all other education was a collective Muslim duty, meaning that if some Muslims did it, the rest were exempted. Like all theoretical debates, it changed form and meaning once it passed through the filter of the individual. It was as an individual that I just scraped through Second Year Secondary, as an individual that I had dreamed from childhood of going to medical school, and as an individual that I knew that there was no second chance on certain experiences, of which taking the Secondary General was one. It was as an individual too that I was aware that, in order to succeed academically, I would need other companions, the old ones with whom my connections had become attenuated since I'd joined the Jama'a and then more or less severed by my transfer from my old school a few months previously. Given the deteriorating Egyptian educational system and the crowding in the schools, there was no alternative to resorting to the private lessons, which were organized in groups of five. There was no alternative either to reserving a place in a group of the highest achievers, so that I didn't end up in the midst of students who took the money from their parents and then spent it on cigarettes, or even of those who went to their lessons but did not spur the teacher to give of his best because he was wasting his time on transferring even the most basic information to a bunch of idiots. I was like an emigrant who returns to a town that has changed toward him and toward which he has changed. The Christians among my old friends would have nothing to do with me and I would have nothing to do with them. The families of my Muslim friends, as the latter eventually told me, were not happy about their being with me in the same study groups because I was a dangerous person who had been removed from his school by the security apparatus only months before. I might still be under surveillance even now. I managed to join some groups that I had chosen and made do with the rest.

The brothers decided that "Islamist action" during the next year should be restrained, to avoid the "disastrous" results of the year before, when we had been transferred to widely scattered schools. Their decision coincided with a whim of my own that made me follow it to the letter. There should be, the Jama'a announced, no violent attempts to change "outrageous behavior," no explicit shows of strength, and no public activities that might attract attention. All that was required of us was to proselytize as individuals and to preserve the Jama'a's existing organizational structure. The 'revolutionary' brothers – and I don't say this to mock them but simply by way of description – were struck with boredom. It became obvious that we were losing ground that we had won before. The activist tendency of the Islamist movement could never be transformed into a mere call for the observance of religious prescriptions. Those who rallied to its banner – like those who rally to the banner of revolutionary movements anywhere in the world – lived on the bread of open opposition and confrontation, no matter what form it might take.

Relief came with the intrepid doings of Baha', who flew through the air and kicked a student at school in his face and, with the other foot, in his chest. When the student tried to run away, Baha' caught him with a scissor-hold round his legs and felled him. After the fight, we discovered that the student who had been beaten had harassed the sister of a friend of Baha''s. Still, it was great to watch, and I felt proud when Baha' stood next to me, or among those who were still keen to attend the circles for proselytization (something that we now did standing, in order not to attract attention). Baha', who had a brown belt in karate, became a star among the brothers, and we'd re-enact the scene at public request, but this time on a group of students who gathered every day to harass the girl students at the school next door.

I, however, had been informed by the school principal that State Security had requested that I be transferred once more, and that he had guaranteed my behavior personally and I was not to let him down. The idea of being moved again was terrifying after my experience of the year before. In any case, it wasn't just the brothers who were fed up with keeping things quiet. There was also a security official, a member of the school administration to whom State Security had assigned the task of keeping order and reporting on any activity that might disturb it. This representative of the security apparatus at our school was black, of huge size, and had bloodshot eyes. He occupied the position of deputy principal and the students called him 'Antar el-Absi.' In a loud voice, he called out, "You, there, you donkey!" I had no previous acquaintance with him, so I thought he must be calling to the Chain Boy, who was walking next to me. However, the man came toward me and punched me in the chest. Without thinking, I punched him back in the face, saying, "Take your hands off me, you asshole!" Then I grabbed him by his shirt and the other students came and separated us, while he shrieked at me that I had to go with him to the principal's office. He left me standing in front of the office while he went in to talk to the principal, and I kept screaming hysterically, "An eye for an eye, you dog! An eye for an eye!" – screams that I took care to make in Classical Arabic as it reminded me of movies about jihad. On some occasions, and this was one of them, hysteria and theatricality are the only solution. They had failed when my knees had betrayed me in front of the boy in our street in the days before I had made my commitment to religion but this time they worked. 'El-Absi' emerged looking quite different than he had when he had gone in. "I am like a father to you," he said, patting me on the shoulder. I, however, brushed away his hand and, looking him in the eye, told him, "You are nothing, and you are worth nothing!" Then I left him and went my way.

The ideas of an eye for an eye and of the blood feud are sacred to those from Egypt's south, that narrow band along the banks of the Nile's narrow thread, far from the plenty of the fertile Delta, and far, too, from any contact with others, be they peaceful visitors or invaders. Had I thought before reacting, I might not have done what I did. I was, after all, threatened with transfer at any moment and was doing everything in my power to avoid such a fate. Also, I had never put myself to the test of a fight, knowing that the result would never be in my favor. At the same time, however, and quite spontaneously, I would feel physically unbearable emotions if anyone insulted me. I would feel my body grow hot, and then the sensation would transform itself into needle pricks in my head. Islam takes this ardor and redirects it, or so I thought, for had I not been committed to the Jama'a Islamiya, and had this man not been aware that he would never get away with it if he exposed me to any mistreatment, he would never have swallowed the insult. God inspires us to be steadfast in situations where others droop, situations, indeed, where we too would droop were we not in His bosom. Anyone of this ilk God would indubitably send victorious, while the other bunch was nothing but a people without a cause, ready to sell themselves at any moment. The incident restored much of my self-confidence, and I felt that the Jama'a, in my person, had regained much of its dignity. But it was all illusion.

The brother responsible for Secondary schools informed me that Secondary School Brothers had met at his house the day before and that they had decided unanimously that I was not up to the mission entrusted to me; therefore I was relieved from now on of leadership of the Secondary School Brothers. I will not pretend that this decision did not have a heavy impact on me. It was, above all, an open declaration of my failure and unsuitability. At the same time, however, it relieved me of a responsibility and gave me the chance to make a 'model' response – a letter that I sent to the same brother, in which I informed him that I accepted the decision, following the example (what conceit!) of the great Muslim general Khalid ibn al-Walid, who had been relieved of the command of the army of Islam while at the height of his conquests. I also referred in the letter to the fact that I had carried out the policy sketched out by the brothers and agreed upon with him personally. It would, therefore, have been more appropriate, if this policy had failed, for him to be fired, not me.

At the same time that I was extricating myself from the responsibilities of overseeing the Islamist action, I was drawing closer on a personal level to some of the students. One of these was the Chain Boy, whose house I would pass by every day to wake him for the dawn prayer. I would stand next to a window of his house and call his name, and I'd feel happy if I heard his sister telling him, "Khaled's calling you" and sad if she said, "Your friend is calling you." At the end of the year before, when I'd reached sixteen, I had asked for her hand in marriage, believing this to be the only successful solution to my obsession with women. As it says in the Hadith, "Young men, let him who is able among you to marry, marry." Her father, however, asked me to wait until I had obtained a university degree that would allow me to get a job. At first, the Chain Boy would come to the Rahma Mosque and we'd chat after the prayer. Later on, however, he told me that he preferred to perform the prayer at a mosque closer to his house. I then went, once, twice, three times, to the same mosque too in order to pray with him but he wasn't there. When I saw him at school, I'd ask him where he'd prayed and he'd give the name of the mosque at which I'd actually prayed. I closeted myself with the Qur'an nonstop for three days, unable to believe that the Chain Boy would lie. He was my first sponsor in the Jama'a and the symbol of courage – which he'd proved inside the Rahma Mosque when it was the target of tear gas shells that made him throw up everything in his stomach. I was sad. I had again this fear of temptation, of a religious test that I might one day fail, thus losing my faith, which would then be replaced in my heart by hypocrisy. When I confronted him, sorrow appeared in his eyes, which never normally shed a tear, so that they looked like wet glass on an early morning. I didn't forgive him for what he had done until he was subjected to a new tribulation. This time, it wasn't enough for State Security to arrest him, they also fabricated a charge of sexual molestation against him, accusing him of seeking to seduce a youth of his own age into performing 'abomination' with him. I followed the progress of the case day by day through the lawyer, who informed us that the youth who had brought the complaint against him was a Christian, and that he, the lawyer, had not allowed the Chain Boy to be subjected to a medical examination by the forensic physician because nothing in the law required that.

I passed with a mark of Outstanding that year, and was first in the whole school (or second, according to some, who claimed that a student who hadn't studied at the school but had just enrolled for the exams had taken first place). I got a high enough score to qualify me easily for medical school. It was a new stage in my life, and in my work for the Islamist cause too. It also brought me a new image in society. "In the name of God, may God protect you! He observed his religion and he did well at school! God is great! God praise the prophet! May God keep him ever so!" people said. I came a step closer to obtaining a star like the one on Rabso's exercise book. He and his brother had come a step closer to Sheikh Tareq, who had asked for their sister's hand. Her wealthy father wouldn't agree, but she insisted. She wanted this pious man at whose hands her younger brothers studied and whom they loved, following him around all day "the way a single baby goat follows its mother," as he used to say jokingly. Years later, I would go my way and the bridal couple would go theirs, to some place of which both I and their family were ignorant. It made a family vulnerable to pressure from the security apparatus to know where their children had fled from the thuggery of the state. God alone can defend the weak.

3

The message revealed

The most attractive thing about Asyut prison is its location, on the Ibrahimiya Canal close to where it leaves the river Nile. At the end of the day, however, it is still a prison. Its huge gate makes anyone standing before it conscious of his insignificance, even if he is only a visitor. We waited our turn. We passed inside through an extremely small inset door where we had to bend down so as not to hit our heads, despite which we were looking forward to going inside. The inmates to be visited that day were the leading brothers, who had been transferred there to sit their exams under the supervision of a special proctoring committee under the University of Asyut, convened inside the prison. Brother Karam Zuhdi, a leader of the military wing of the organization that killed Sadat and attempted to stage a coup against the regime in 1981 and who had been sentenced to life imprisonment, was there, as was Asem Abd el-Majed, a member of the Command Council who had taken part in the same events and lost his knee, which meant that he couldn't walk properly; his lot was also life imprisonment. With Asem Dirbala, he was one of the two most prominent writers of the Jama'a's thoughts and statements. There were other brothers too whom I hadn't met.

This was the first time for me to meet Sheikh Karam and Sheikh Asem face to face; on the same occasion I would also meet Sheikh Mahmud Shu'eib, who had been in detention for several months. The encounter made me happy, despite the gloomy atmosphere that hung over the visit as a result of the death of one of the brother detainees who had been given a shot of penicillin that his body had rejected. I had been asked, before going to visit the brothers, to write an overview of Islamist action inside the Secondary schools to show to these leading figures, and I'd written down thirteen detailed points, among them a scathing critique of the older brother who was in charge of us. This I had sent via some brothers who had visited earlier. I was looking forward to hearing the brothers' response.

I wore a white polo shirt tucked inside my pants and not hanging down outside, as when one wears European clothes. I met Sheikh Mahmud first and he said to me laughingly as he shook my hand, "What's all this you've done to yourself?" – not just because of my clothes but also my hairstyle. It was short but the front was a little longer than the rest and combed forward and to the right. I'd expected there'd be comments but I didn't want to neglect, when visiting these senior figures, something that I did from time to time in my ordinary life. The brothers would sometimes allude to the care I took to make my clothes elegant, but they didn't disparage me for that. There was something that drew me more to the brothers who dressed well than to those who did not. A trivial matter, I'm sure you'll agree, but a part of what I was. I once got talking to a brother who had entered medical school two years before me; he was executed, God rest his soul, after taking part in the assassination of Ref'at el-Mahjub. He told me that he needed a quarter of an hour from the time he got out of bed to when he left the house, and I said that I needed half an hour just to look in the mirror and change from one outfit into another. He smiled and said, "Just don't forget to say the prayer for looking at yourself in the mirror!" I didn't stop taking care over my clothes, but I also took greater care to say that prayer, which goes, "Thanks be to God that what is unpleasant in others he has made pleasant in me." Sheikh Mahmud told me that Sheikh Asem Abd el-Majed had praised the paper I'd submitted. When he presented me to Sheikh Asem, the latter looked laughingly at Sheikh Mahmud and said, "And tall too!" Then he looked questioningly at me and asked, "Can you run?" I informed him that I'd been on the soccer team when I was young and he said, "Excellent, excellent."

This banter was in reference to the physical attributes required of those chosen to take part in jihadist operations. The most important among these were the characteristics of faith, good morals, and a strong personality. I knew that if it were up to Sheikh Mahmud, he would recommend that I be chosen as one

of that select band: another brother had passed on to me something that Sheikh Mahmud had said of me, to the effect that "If I
had ten like Khaled, I could overturn the regime." In any case, I
was now going to be presented to the commander-in-chief, Karam
Zuhdi, who, in 1981, had transported weapons from place to place,
stopping at several points along the road to change the color of
the vehicle. The brothers always spoke of the piercing gaze that he
would direct into the eyes of the person he was speaking with and
which made it impossible for the latter to hide anything that was
in his heart. This was what I was looking at now.

My lot of that piercing look lasted for no more than a minute,
and I had nothing in my heart that I wanted to hide, but it was
enough for me to be sure that Sheikh Asem's joking was just that: if
the brothers had chosen me for a jihadist mission, Sheikh Karam
would have spoken with me for longer than that. In fact, I didn't
feel worthy. The things of this world still occupied a part of my
heart. My obedience waxed at certain times but waned at others.
This was not just at the level of not staying up all night in prayer
but even at that of performing my basic religious duties, such the
dawn prayer. This was no small matter. The first criterion that
the brothers used in choosing people for jihadist missions was
the candidate's degree of observance of his duties of worship. All
the brothers who had taken part in jihadist missions had been of
the type of whom stories of nightlong devotions and continuous
fasting circulated. Below this was another level of obedience, that
known as "hearing and obeying," by which was meant unquestion-
ing obedience to the orders of your immediate superior. I don't
believe that, for a religious group that obeyed its Creator first and
the orders of that Creator's representatives second, the two of them
were truly separate, for "hearing and obeying" was like an unbro-
ken chain extending from the heavens to the earth. For example,
Brother M.M. had stuck leaflets on walls and the police had fired
on him and those with him, so he fled. When he returned to headquarters, it was the decision of the brothers that he should return
to the same place and resume his work, which he did immediately.
Following this minor incident, M.M. was chosen for a jihadist
mission even though he was an 'obscure' brother whom no one

had heard of before. Who was I in comparison to someone like him? My father described me as a rebel, and I loved that description, which I saw as representing a praiseworthy characteristic. When, however, I was described the same way by members of the Jama'a, such as Sheikh Tareq and Sheikh Usama, who were each at different times my immediate superiors, it certainly placed me in a blameworthy category. "Hearing and obeying" was an expression that had been carefully crafted to perform the shift from an act of reception – hearing – to one of implementation – obeying – with nothing in the middle to make it, for example, "hearing and being convinced and obeying." I tried to recall the number of times on which I had demonstrated a great capacity to hear and obey, but I couldn't think of any. There had been the time that I'd broken the bottle of alcohol, but that had been an inappropriate kind of hearing and obeying because it had been done without permission from anyone in authority. Sometimes when I was moving Jama'a publications from a nearby printing press on my bicycle in a large cardboard box, I'd place it on the back seat and tie it on with an old bicycle inner tube. True, this activity contained an element of danger, but I discovered later that many others had done it and that I had been chosen primarily because of my youth, and because my face was still beardless and unknown to the security services, meaning that I was unlikely to be stopped.

A few days later, I was visited at home by a brother whom I knew to be involved in underground work. While we were talking, he asked me what I was hoping to do in the Jama'a. I told him I wanted to become a martyr – a standard response, rather than a truth convincing to me or to him, the experienced brother. He didn't comment but he didn't visit me again. Later, I agreed to go to the faculty housing compound at the university to visit Ahmad, who had been complicit in my expulsion from the compound, with a brother in the medical school. We were to distribute presents to those who were about to enter the school so as to open channels of communication with them. My only condition was that we go there at night, and the brother agreed without knowing the reason for my request – namely that I was going over in my mind the scene in which I had left that place crying some years before, and ridden my bike back to the house while I whispered to myself over and over, "You bastards. You bastards." I ran into Ahmad's mother, who was also a teacher at the medical school, below their building. I said hello to her and told her why we had come. She said that Ahmad was away but her husband was there. I thanked God that I wouldn't have to see him in his house again. We went up to their apartment and gave his father Ahmad's gift. Going to prison was easier for me than going into that place, and that is a fact, not a figure of speech.

I didn't go to campus the first day. One could only laugh at the joy of the new students with their new life. Insignificant things, however, have a way of turning into big issues for no good reason in the eyes of those who have no larger cause to concern themselves with. My ultimate dream was to escape the school walls and the authority of the teachers, and that I had done. In any case, I was obliged to go to campus the very next day, as I was informed by colleagues that "the sons of the professors" had taken their seats in the places where, by tradition, only female students sat. There were three forbidden things that we would not give way to: male and female students sitting next to one another in the lecture hall, the presence of both sexes at practical classes, and direct conversation between a male and a female student. Before going to speak to the male students who had taken their places directly behind the rows of girls, I wanted to make sure that there were unoccupied places in the rest of the huge lecture hall, so that they would have no excuse. As I entered, I raised my eyes to the amphitheater and couldn't see where it ended. One thousand two hundred individuals of my size formed a human pyramid mounting in serried ranks. One thousand two hundred heads, one thousand two hundred pairs of eyes looking in one direction. Was it possible that all of them would undertake to do what I was going to ask of them? I wished that the professors' sons hadn't done what they had and that they had spontaneously observed what they knew to be the practice, thus sparing me from having to start a confrontation in front of all those eyes. I climbed up to the highest tier. The last two rows were still completely empty and the loudspeakers ensured that the lecturer's voice would reach everyone. All that one might object to was that the stage seemed a long way away and that the features of the professor standing there would not be clearly distinguishable. Some brothers gave lectures in the university amphitheaters. How brave they must be!

I was seventeen years old when I began my university studies in 1989; a shy person, who preferred to read, write, and discuss more than to speak in front of a crowd. The Jama'a had tried to turn me into a public speaker by training me to exercise that skill in front of small groups selected from among the brothers, but I had failed twice. I was unable to maintain the flow of my ideas and continuity of the sermon. I would forget and my saliva would dry up and I'd stammer. The first time, I kept speaking by force of will, as though talking to myself. The second time, however, I gripped my stomach and made the excuse that it was hurting and stopped completely.

Sheikh Mahmud, with his sharp tongue, made bitter fun of me, putting his hand on his stomach every time he saw me and repeating the words I'd used: "My stomach is hurting." He stopped engaging me in serious conversation as he had used to and contented himself with giving me a terse greeting. Immediately following this incident we were at the Jam'iya Shar'iya preparing for the summer camp, during which we would spend a whole week inside the mosque, watching jihadist videotapes, receiving two or three concentrated lessons daily, and spending the night in devotions. Sheikh Mahmud charged me with the job of sorting the donated clothing by kind, excluding me from the tasks that required special skills, such as writing the leaflets that we would distribute, putting together the program, or coming up with ideas for activities. He took me to the mosque's inner room and showed me a pile of clothes, then went out and closed the door on me. When he came back to see what I'd done, he found me doing what he had asked of me and crying like a child that had been forbidden to take part in a family activity. The prominent leader, sweet-tongued preacher, and relative by marriage of both Sheikh Umar

Abd el-Rahman and Sheikh Karam Zuhdi, upset to see me in this state, kissed my head and my hands in apology, and fussed about, unable to decide what to do to make me happy. From then on, I started writing out sermons and learning them by heart, then standing for hours in front of the mirror and delivering them. Afterward I would go to the mosque when there was nobody there, climb the steps of the pulpit, and repeat the same sermon. I would imagine myself standing before the congregation, preaching and leading marches. I would shout till my face turned red and stamp the ground with my foot. I made every effort I was capable of but never acquired the ability to stand up in front of people and deliver a sermon.

Now, when I saw all those people in the amphitheater, I knew for sure that public speaking was not for me. I did, however, get excited about what I had to do. I went straight to the row on the right hand side of the hall where the professors' sons were sitting behind the girls. Resolutely I informed them that what they were doing was wrong and that, starting the next day, they were to sit with the other male students in the middle or bear the consequences. Thank God, they did so. This was the least I could do at the university, and from now on, I decided, I would take my role seriously. Once, I forbade a male student from talking to a female student, and he told me she was his twin sister. "Even if that's true," I told him very calmly, "people such as myself cannot know that you are siblings."

The mixing of the sexes was the source of all corruption, and no excuses for it could be accepted. Standing at the door of the mosque, I watched a group of brothers stop a foreign boy and girl who were walking together in the street. They told them to go separate ways, and the girl cried, saying in English that she didn't know the town and couldn't walk about in it on her own. The brothers, nonetheless, insisted. When the boy tried to object, they pushed him and told him to walk away in the direction they chose for him. I couldn't understand how the two of them would meet up again, given that the brothers had chosen the path that each was to take, but I also understood that this was the right thing to do, and God's law took precedence over what humans might believe. That was what a brother had said when he had been given the task of "changing what is forbidden" with regard to a man who used to commit fornication with a woman when her husband was at Friday prayer. The brothers dragged the two of them out of the house in which they practiced their scandalous acts and beat them severely. The physician brother, who would go with them when they wanted to "change what is forbidden" without that leading to death, transgressed God's law and his own personal role by yelling at the brothers, "Cover them up! 'God is a covering for His slaves.'" Brother Ala', who told me this story and who was my amir at the university, yelled back at him God's law as it was laid down in the Qur'an: "*Scourge each one of them a hundred stripes … and let a party of the believers witness their chastisement*" (God has spoken truly) (Qur'an 24:2). Today, mixing of the sexes among foreigners, or among Muslim men and women, and tomorrow who knew what might not occur? Who would have expected that two Christian men would have dared to have sex with two female Muslim university students? The brothers didn't hesitate when it came to those two. They beat one of them to death and broke the other's back, then cut off one of his ears. If such mixing had been prevented in its initial stages, things would never have got to this point. As custodians of the society, as guardians of its morals, as those who sought its good, this was our special role.

It was not, however, our only role, for we also tried, in so far as it was in our power, to correct social inequities. We took it upon ourselves to collect the lectures, copy them at a print shop, and sell them to the students at affordable prices. We also brought order to the entry and exit of the students into and out of the lecture hall and ensured a supply of skeleton parts so that those students who were unable to afford them could use them in their studies. Since the cost of one complete skeleton normally was equal to two months of a government employee's salary, the students of modest means, the people who were just 'scraping by,' and who had no 'in' to make everything easy, were grateful for this service, and grateful to us. They knew we were doing something for them that they couldn't do for themselves.

I was on my way to the mosque to pray the evening prayer

when Sheikh Khaled met me. He was a brother who had served a seven-year prison sentence in the Sadat assassination case. He asked me in a tone of annoyance, "Aren't you going to make a bit more of an effort?" Sheikh Mahmud was standing next to him and I understood straightaway what he meant. Instead of entering the mosque, I went straight to a small mosque I knew, on the ground floor of a building on the road between my house and my old school. There I distractedly prayed the evening prayer, then forced myself, as though pushing a refrigerator on wheels, to go and stand next to the imam, and launched into the sermon that I'd been practicing on in the privacy of my own room. It was about the meaning of the word 'man' in the Noble Qur'an. I spoke like a schoolchild repeating a text after the teacher. I couldn't move my hands as I was supposed to, or control the expression on my face and the register of my voice. All the same, the experience encouraged me and I repeated it in other small mosques. I even plucked up my courage and delivered the same sermon after the afternoon prayer at the Rahma Mosque, the brothers' second most important, with the amir of the Jama'a, Sheikh Ahmad Abduh, sitting right before me in the first row.

When I mounted the stage and took the professor's position in the amphitheater at the university, I almost fainted. With the spine of a notebook that was in my hand, I banged on the table. I had convinced myself, and strange to say had become convinced, that this was all I had to do. If the noise had been disquieting, the silence was frightening, and left me exposed. I began my sermon. The students listened for a few minutes and then the noise started again. I ended up in effect preaching to myself and was saved only by the entrance of the professor. Preaching, I consoled myself, wasn't the only means of proselytization. A person might be moved by a sermon and then forget everything he'd heard five minutes later. Personal proselytization – focusing on specific individuals – had an ongoing effect. In the hands of the brothers, it had been transformed into a programmed activity that we called "softening the hearts" – meaning softening them through gifts and visits to people's homes and to the sick, through a kind word and a smile. The important thing, though, was to choose the right individuals, because this method could not rely on random meetings of minds, as might be the case in ordinary circumstances, but had to be subject each time to a simple 'feasibility study.' Thus someone who was well-spoken, well organized in his daily routine, family-oriented, and obedient to his parents would always be sympathetic, but would never go beyond that limit. The ardent individual, however, who loved adventure and harbored a deep sense of resentment, would be more likely to commit himself, if he showed any understanding of our cause. None of these matters was clearly delimited, and may be simply a reflection of my own vision, right or wrong, of myself and of the idea that I'd formed early on that the Islamist movement was a movement of the resentful middle class, the medical school being the clearest expression of this idea. True, the greater number of the movement's followers were from among the poor, but most of the leaders of the Jama'a were from families with a goodly apportionment of education but a shaky apportionment of money and/or authority. The only problem with personal proselytization was that it was exhausting, reached limited numbers, and didn't have the moral authority of preaching.

I tried once more. I started my sermon and the voices of the students rose as before. I was ready, though. I stopped speaking and looked directly at the individuals and groups who were holding conversations on the side. Then I said, in the colloquial, "When you stop talking when I am speaking, you are not being silent out of respect for me. No. You are being silent out of respect for God's word and His Messenger." The students then fell as silent as if I'd performed a miracle in front of them. The best thing to do was to stop right there. The next time I would be ready and would start again at the beginning. I left the podium and went back to my place in the amphitheater, refusing to go on with my sermon. Thenceforth, no one spoke when I preached. The attentiveness encouraged me. I started branching out into new topics. One day, a love letter from a male student to a female fell into my hands and I read it out to the students from the stage and we laughed together at the naivety of the style and the superficiality of the sentiments it expressed. This gave me an opening to talk about the mixing of the sexes, its harmful effects, and Islam's ruling on it. My next sermon was aimed at a boy and girl student who had dated near our house. Then we moved on to another stage. I would memorize terms from the books of Sayyid Qutb and Muhammad Qutb such as 'totem,' 'taboo,' 'ego,' and 'super ego' and make a point of using them in my sermons, or I would read a chapter about the three Jews, Marx, Durkheim, and Freud, so that I could talk in my sermon about the Jewish conspiracy to sabotage human thought.

I requested from the brothers that a portion of the budget be set aside for the girls, because they exercised an indirect influence on their siblings and on their families, and Brother Esam told me, "But we want people who can bear arms." He was right, but all the same I gave a book to one of the female students after she alone of all of them volunteered to collect the money for the model exam aides-mémoire that the Jama'a was printing for the students. I also presented a book to another girl after I learned that she had objected to a quarrel that almost led to blows between us and the Muslim Brotherhood, the book accompanied by a letter in my own handwriting in which I explained the reasons for what had happened, after which she replied with a letter in which she set out her point of view. This exchange of letters took place in the manner usually used between me and the female students: I would identify with a quick glance where the girl was and then put whatever it was I wanted in front of her without addressing her directly. In this case, however, even this quick glance was enough for the girl to captivate me with her eyes.

I had started liking medical school, but would that help now? We heard heavy gunfire and panicked and tried to flee the mosque. Chaotic attempts at escape were accompanied by cries from here and there, indistinctly mingled sounds that were more screams than words. The sounds of bullets close by made my body quake. Our escape route to the outside world was narrow, and bodies cannoned into one another in front of it, then pushed and shoved like old pastry under a rusty mincing knife. Things got worse when two brothers ran to the door of the mosque and closed it with an iron bar on the inside while the brothers in charge shouted at us not to flee in this disorganized manner and to listen to their instructions. We all knew that "hearing and obeying" in such circumstances is of the greatest importance and that we had to have military discipline, but we weren't trained, by which I mean that we hadn't been trained by being put through rehearsals of the real thing. Our heads contained a certain amount of theoretical information that we had to download in the current circumstances. And all of this was taking place in a mosque I had never been in before, the Great Mosque in the West Town district.

A few weeks after the start of my first academic year, the security forces surrounded the Jam'iya Shar'iya mosque and prevented the brothers from praying there. They also carried out a huge campaign of arrests that swept up most of the leaders of the Jama'a, while those who were not caught went into hiding. We were not allowed to hold our regular meeting after evening prayer on Mondays. It was the most violent and widest campaign by the security forces against the brothers since I had become one of them. Despite this, the Jama'a insisted on continuing its work and on continuing its Monday meetings, whatever the cost. We would hold the meeting in a different mosque each week, and we changed the time from after the evening prayer to after the sunset prayer. The security of the meeting was guaranteed by the 'brothers on bikes,' a band of activists, clean shaven, whose task was to inform the members of the Jama'a, a little while ahead, where the meeting would be held and then to watch the roads leading to the place and provide an escape route for the brothers should they be forced to flee. More precise still was the security provided for the arrival and departure of the brother who was going to preach at the meeting. Esam was one of these activist brothers. We had a bond in our love of soccer, and he was always careful to watch the matches, in the face of the ultra-puritanism of some of the brothers, who proscribed such things. He had wide eyes with equally pointed eyebrows that gave him a permanently inquiring expression. I would joke with him that he was the only person in the world whom I knew to be cleverer than me. Esam had only a few hairs on his chin and two lines of hair where his sideburns should be – physical characteristics that added to his other, moral, qualities to make of him the ideal jihadist. More than a year later, he took part in the assassination of the speaker of the People's Assembly, Ref'at el-Mahjub, and was the last of those who had carried out the operation to remain at large. Motorcycles going against the flow of the traffic provided the element of surprise that allowed him and the other members of the group to carry out the assassination without any of them being wounded.

Despite the skills deployed and the precautions taken, the plans to ensure the security of the mosques in Asyut were not entirely successful. Thus it happened that we now found ourselves besieged inside the Great Mosque. I leaned my back against the wall, looking at the ground and weighing up the difficult options. When the door was closed, I realized that I would not be called upon to exercise any of these right away; indeed, they would be preceded by a dish of teargas shells in a closed space, followed by retching and vomiting. I recalled all the things I'd heard about similar situations. Then the leader yelled at us to escape via the door of the back patio of the mosque. To do so, we had to go to the upper floor, then climb down the wall as there was no direct route to the outer door from there. I went to the upper floor and looked down between my feet. I could see no way to descend the wall, and the distance to the ground was too far to jump without risk of breaking one's legs. Once again, I had a fleeting thought of brothers who had been observed fleeing from the Jam'iya Shar'iya in similar circumstances: they had jumped to the ground in a resilient posture, one we called a 'spring,' which involved bending the knees so that, as soon as their feet touched the ground, with their heels tucked in and touching their backsides, they could get up and run. I looked down once more, my legs trembling. A brother called to me to jump, while behind me was the sound of bullets, each of which I imagined was aimed at me. I plucked up my courage and jumped, in the approved posture. Then I got up and ran through the door, through rustic houses and passageways with which I was unfamiliar, in a poor neighborhood called al-Qaysariya, albeit in the vernacular the name was pronounced el-Esariya (in the dialect of Cairo) or el-Gesariya (in that of Upper Egypt). Because these pronunciations were similar to the word we use to describe the 'potty' that young children urinate into, I had always believed that the name referred to the fact that the district was poor; some of its houses were built of unbaked mud brick like those of villages. I stopped, not knowing which direction to take or where to go and scared to head back the way I had come, to where the security forces were massed. I had forgotten that I had shaved my beard off the week before so that I could go onto campus, which I hadn't visited for an entire month. A woman aged about forty caught sight of me, hurried over, took me by the hand, and hid me in one of the small chicken coops that exist among the houses. I sat down, frightened, and peering expectantly and tensely out through the wire, but thinking too about the woman who had taken my hand. Should I have taken hold of hers or not? Was there a big enough difference in age between her and me for that to be permissible?

The Jama'a Islamiya had opened up new horizons for me in my rebellion against the typical petit bourgeois upbringing that I had received at home and at school and caused me to submerge myself in the life of different social classes as a natural outcome of missionary work. This placed me in an independent category that neither belonged to any of these classes nor sought to do so. Thus I would give alms to a certain youth with six brothers and sisters for whom he was the sole provider, even though he himself was only seventeen. He also had his expenses as a student at the Azhar Institute to find. When I did so, I'd feel good about myself. I'd also listen to the romantic adventures of a student who had lived for a year in Hungary, where he had gone to study medicine because his marks in the Secondary General exam didn't qualify him to study it in Egypt. This young man was forced to face a new reality when his mother, a university professor whose husband had died a few years previously, remarried. Whenever they fought, his mother would remind him that he had spent seventy thousand pounds during his year in Hungary. He couldn't stand his life anymore and feared that he might offend God, especially with girls, who were attracted to him without the slightest effort on his part, he being one of those who "believes from the depths of his being" and who would weep whenever he listened to the Qur'an. I had no idea what I could do for him, so I went to Sheikh Tal'at Yasin and told him the story. The sheikh frowned as he declared that he "sought refuge with God from such people." If only he'd had seventy thousand pounds, he said, he'd have overturned the Egyptian regime. He then warned me that the best thing I could do was to keep away from such people as no good was to be hoped for from them. Their tales, he added, might seduce my heart, distracting me with the sort of nonsense that preoccupied the affluent classes.

When things had calmed down a bit, the same woman came back and took me to her house, where the rest of her family was having a meal and drinking tea. They greeted me and invited me to eat, something for which I naturally had not the slightest desire. I drank tea with them and they suggested they fetch me a razor so that I could shave my beard, which was starting to sprout. I thanked them, however, and refused, explaining that in its present state it was small cause for alarm. Then a young man from the family took me to a wall and told me that if I climbed over it I could get to a safe place from which I could return to our house. Thus, on the very first day of 1990, I escaped arrest.

About a month after the raid on the Great Mosque, the trouble came to an end. Some brothers were released from prison and we were permitted to hold our seminars and the Friday prayer, though in the Rahma Mosque and not at the Jam'iya Shar'iya mosque. It was like a dream, a rehearsal for the great victory that was, inevitably, coming, a lesson in remaining patient until relief from distress should be provided. So I would say to Esam as we helped one another shake out a carpet in front of the Rahma Mosque, each of us holding one of its ends as it rose and then fell again, hiding and then revealing his smiling face. I felt as though I was cleaning a house after a period of mourning and announcing the return to normal life. The Jama'a, especially after this period of trouble and after I'd once performed an experiment on myself by shaving off my beard, had become my life. I thought about the Jama'a a great deal, but from within, and never heretically, in such a way as to question the reasons for its existence. On a personal level, my greatest loss was the brothers who went to prison and also the impossibility of my sitting the midyear exams. At the same time, the above-mentioned shaving of my beard, which had begun rapidly covering my face during the summer vacation before I went to college, was also a cruel lesson. When I returned to the amphitheater for the first time, I used a scarf to cover the place where my beard had been, like the actor Mahmud el-Meligi in *el-Ard* (The Land), when the agents of colonialism shave off his mustache in an attempt to humiliate him. It was also difficult for me to accept looking like everyone else in any mosque I might attend, and to know that the people there, standing in their rows to pray and waiting for one of their number to come forward and lead the prayer, would not look at me and say, "Please go ahead, Sheikh," as had been the case when I had had a beard. And once, shaven, I went up to a youth who was talking to a girl on campus and asked him to stop it. Instead of apologizing and making some excuse, as had usually happened before, he looked at me contemptuously and said, "Who do you think you are?"

At the end of the year, I had to retake exams in three subjects out of four. I was lucky in that our school allowed one to repeat any number of subjects during the summer vacation. Things were not, however, as easy as I imagined they would be. This first academic failure of my life made me taste humiliation, before the friends of my childhood and also before a female fellow student with whom, toward the end of the year, I'd started talking on the telephone. She told me that she was convinced that I was an outstanding individual and that she had been shocked at the result. She said this by way of praise, but her arrow missed its mark.

Sheikh Ammar (not his real name) took me to his apartment and asked me to conceal myself in an inner room so that I could overhear and bear witness to the investigation of the Chain Boy. Then he left again and returned to the apartment, bringing the latter with him. He didn't let him know that there was a third person present. The Chain Boy denied the charge that had been made against him, which was, in essence, based on information transmitted to the brothers by neighbors of his who were not themselves above suspicion, and who were so well known for smoking hashish and drinking alcohol that the brothers had earlier considered disciplining them. The charges, however, were too grave to be ignored, especially as earlier accusations existed to reinforce them.

A year before, the brothers had asked me to go to a small mosque that they supervised on Nemeis Street. When I went, I found a number of brothers filling the mosque. I didn't know why I'd been invited, and many others, I think, who had gone there didn't know why they'd been either. When we had formed rows for the prayer, we found a well-known member of the Brothers of '81 – I'll call him Sheikh S. – who was celebrated in particular for his unrivaled courage, insisting on leading the prayer, while three of the brothers, chains in hand, were preventing him and ordering him to leave the mosque and never return. They insisted instead that another brother lead the prayer. Sheikh S. was known to be an advocate of armed confrontation with the regime as the only possible course of action and, or so I supposed, must have joined another group, one that adopted this approach, and the brothers must therefore not want him as an imam in a mosque belonging to the Jama'a Islamiya. However, I was wrong.

The alternative imam, who was a leader of the first rank in the Jama'a, warned Sheikh S. time after time not to persevere in refusing to leave the mosque, but the latter refused to acquiesce. The leader argued with Sheikh S. more than once, using language that gave the impression that Sheikh S. knew why he had to leave, but without elaboration. Then the Jama'a leader ordered us to sit (I was in the second row) and gave a signal to two brothers, who advanced on the 'disgraced' brother – the one who was so well known for his bravery – and beat him up. In seconds, as in a scene from a movie, blood was trickling down the wall behind Sheikh S., who lay motionless on the ground. The brother sitting next to me put out his hand and placed it on my knee to stop it shaking. Some brothers carried the banished man, more dead than alive, out of the mosque, I don't know where to, for the brothers took me outside too, after I started crying, so that I wouldn't affect those around me, and I didn't see him there. In the short intervening interval, the Jama'a leader had informed us that the man who had been thrown out was a sodomite and that he deserved worse than that, since the rule in Islam was that such a person should be thrown to his death from a high place. Now, the same accusation had been made against the Chain Boy.

I tried to figure out on my own what had happened in a way that I could understand. This man who had been disgraced was a prominent member of the Jama'a, and his courage, despite his short stature, was proverbial throughout the group. How, then, could he end up like that? Could the reason be his torture in Egypt's prisons? I had read the details of the case he brought against the State Security apparatus in an opposition newspaper. The forensic evidence had proved that his backside had been violated by the insertion of a stick, and my information regarding homosexuality was that someone who had had an object inserted in his backside would thereafter feel an emptiness that he would want to fill. All the same, I could not overcome the shock that I felt. Until that instant, I had believed that we were an angelic society, one that resembled the first cohort of the Companions of the Prophet, whom Sayyid Qutb referred to as a "peerless qur'anic generation." This incident punched a hole through the picture I'd built up in my mind's eye concerning this society. When I got to the point where I felt I couldn't make sense of the matter on my own, I told the leader brother who had given the order for him to be beaten up that I couldn't take in what had happened to Sheikh S. "First of all," responded the brother, "don't say 'Sheikh S.' He's 'that boy S.'" Then he explained to me how Islamic society had never been a society of angels. Even in the days of the Prophet, there had been Companions who had committed adultery, which is why God had stipulated a punishment for it. Another Companion had committed high treason by revealing the secrets of the Muslims to the unbelievers. Had God not known that Islamic society would contain sodomites, He would not have stipulated a punishment for sodomy. The difference, he went on, between Islamic society and other societies was that Islamic society struck at the hands of those who violated its laws and expelled them from its ranks, thus preventing the spread of abomination among the believers. He ended by saying, "The important thing is that you don't feel any compassion for these sinners."

The incident didn't make me feel revulsion toward the Jama'a Islamiya. On the contrary, it made me prouder of it still. I understood the matter from the perspective of a Hadith of the Prophet's that says, "By Him in whose hand the soul of Muhammad is held, should Fatima the daughter of Muhammad steal, I would cut off her hand!" At the same time, however, I needed a shock like that to grasp that we were not saints, innocent of all major sins, and that, as individuals, we were capable of committing more than peccadilloes. A sin of such magnitude had never occurred to me. We were, as far as I was concerned, a pearl in the necklace of light that extended through Islamic history; we were not simply a part of that history, but one of its historic, or, to be more precise, of its critical and defining, moments.

I never spoke of this episode to anyone in the Jama'a again. I didn't even tell the Chain Boy until a year later, or a few days before the events I am now describing. He hadn't heard about it, or so he told me, and his eyes immediately filled with those tears of his that never actually fell, and I reproached myself for having caused him pain, especially after the case that State Security had concocted against him regarding the Christian boy. We also touched on other rumors that involved a brother who was older than us and had been hit by a bullet in the leg. The reason I believed this particular rumor was that this brother had a special stance when he played ping-pong that involved his sticking his backside out. This reasoning in turn sprang from another widespread belief in our society to the effect that people with large buttocks were 'faggots,' because the insertion of the male member into their buttocks inflated them. My father also used to tell me, when I was young, that we – the men folk of the al-Berry family – were famous for the small size of our buttocks. Naturally, I know neither the orbit nor the extent of this reputation, nor why it would be of any interest to others that our buttocks were small, nor under what circumstances others had vouchsafed their belief that our buttocks were

small, but, in any case, I took 'smallness of buttock' to be something that men ought to be proud of, and this naive belief reflected
itself in my mind onto the image of that poor young man, with the
result that I immediately believed that he was one of "the people
of Lot," even though there wasn't the slightest evidence to prove it.

My friendship with the Chain Boy was too strong for me to
apply this 'posterior' wisdom to him directly, even though he too
had prominent and well-rounded buttocks, which were particularly obvious when he wore his form-fitting white Saudi jallabiya.
In addition, he was fair-skinned, which was another characteristic
that in our local lore did not fit well with true manliness. I had
been his friend for close to three years and had noticed nothing
suspicious about him. Despite this, after Sheikh Ammar had pres-
sured him with details, he confessed that the accusations against
him were true. His relationship with the neighbor of his in question had begun two years before, in the days of the Usama ibn Zayd
Club, before the security forces had expelled the brothers from the
Jam'iya Shar'iya mosque. He said it had happened the first time at
a moment when the brothers were busy with the afternoon prayer,
and that he'd made the first move by asking the other boy if the
rumors that he did it with men were true. The best thing the Chain
Boy said that day was that none of the brothers had ever done it
with him, though he did add, "I think, though, that some of them
wanted to." Sheikh Ammar responded, "That's because you've got
a dirty mind and think that everyone wants to fuck you."

When the interrogation was over, the Chain Boy came out
and I heard him pleading with his interrogator not to tell anyone
about what had happened. Then Sheikh Ammar came back into
the apartment, closed the door, and told me, "Damn him! The lady
who lives next to us was opening her door as he said, 'Don't tell
anyone.'" Then he added, "It's good that you were here. That one
(meaning the Chain Boy) is possessed by the Devil." Soon after
that, when the outcome of the interrogation had become common
knowledge, one of the leading brothers made the comment, "It'd
be a disaster if the Chain Boy was the passive one, even with that
Christian boy" (referring to the earlier case, which we had previously believed State Security had made up to get him).

At this point I was living on my own most of the time in an apartment directly below my parents', where I was reviewing for the make-up exams. I received the Chain Boy in a room with a north-facing window where I would sleep and study in the August heat. I told him, untruthfully, that the brothers had recorded his confessions and I had listened to the tape. I was sitting on a single bed facing the window and next to the door and he was sitting on a single bed next to the window and facing the door. Two tables with wheels that I'd brought down with me from our apartment and a wooden chair on which I'd put two cushions, one as a seat and the other as a backrest, separated us. He told me that he'd done what he did with one of the students at our Secondary school, where, together, we'd initiated our Islamist action. It had started with them bumping into one another on the staircase in the midst of a throng of students, and come to its conclusion at the other boy's house. "How could that be?" I asked him. "Wasn't he living with his family?" The reply was that they'd let their pants down and do it standing up, one of them bending over a chair that they would place against the door of the main room to ensure that no one burst in on them. I felt something liquid in my underpants and could feel my member throbbing. He'd done what he wanted and got away with it, and I had no doubt he'd do it again and again, and with whom? With men! If he'd wanted to try to tempt me, he could have done so, nothing stood in his way; and if he didn't want to, he wouldn't. I, on the other hand, was not able to touch a woman, because that was forbidden. Or because I wouldn't take a risk, the way he had – I wasn't capable of putting my reputation and my image to the test. He could behave like Zuleikha, the wife of the King of Egypt in the Qur'an, but I would never be able to claim that I had done as Yusuf did. "Did you wear a nightie?" I asked him. "Did they tell you, 'Bend over, girl!?'" Those sodomites were without shame and deserved the punishment of execution by being cast from a high place that God had set for them. Why didn't he show the appropriate degree of regret as I directed these slights at him? Why wasn't he weeping before me? Why hadn't Sheikh S. collapsed, minimized the scandal, and left the mosque instead of exposing himself to abuse and being thrown out after a beating?

The Chain Boy told me that he'd thought more than once about committing suicide out of chagrin and sorrow over this disease with which he was smitten. He explained it by saying that when he was in the Gulf, where he had spent several years as a child, men had done it to him, so he'd grown accustomed to it. He told me too that he'd tried without success to divert himself from this interest by practicing sports, fasting, and spending time at the mosque. I don't know if he was telling the truth or not, but I was very affected by his deep sense of guilt. The brothers had secularized the way they dealt with him and sent him to a psychiatrist, even though the Jama'a did not regard, or deal with, homosexuality as a phenomenon capable of being cured but as a sin that rendered the one who committed it liable to punishment. It then became my job, subsequently, to give him the pill that the brother doctor had prescribed for him and which they told me would kill his sexual appetite. He would come to me every day at nine in the evening to take the pill and I wouldn't be able to look him in the face. The Chain Boy never left the Jama'a Islamiya, even though he was asked not to come to the mosque. He insisted, however, on coming. When they greeted him, the brothers would no longer embrace him as they would have done ordinarily but this did not discourage him. Even compelling him to come to me daily to take the pill I regarded as excessively humiliating but he accepted the sentence uncomplainingly, neither rebelling nor objecting, and never saying, "Leave me be, since you know I'm not worthy of being welcomed within the ranks of your group." He had violated a clear law of Islam, a violation whose punishment supposedly was to be cursed and expelled from the mercy of God, and he still didn't leave the Jama'a. I wanted only one thing: that he would insist on taking the pill himself each day and not come to me. I was afraid that I'd wake up one day and find out that he'd committed suicide; then I'd never be able to forgive myself. The dead body of Sheikh S. was discovered in a field in a village near Asyut. The Chain Boy, though, was arrested with the brothers in 1992 and remained in prison without trial for twelve years.

I started to fear for myself more. I felt that the snares of Satan were closer to humankind than was commonly believed. I still committed my "petty sins." From time to time I'd revert to watching girls through the shutters and I'd talk on the phone to a female colleague to whom I had no legitimate connection – talking on the phone being a state of "semi-privacy" that was only permitted in cases of extreme urgency. They were just short conversations and to the point at first, but little by little they stretched into hours, the topics ranging from one thing to another. Things even reached the point at which I confided to her that I loved (though I used terms that avoided the word 'love,' such as 'admired' or 'wished to form a relationship with') a friend of hers – the girl, to be precise, with whom I had exchanged messages concerning the quarrel between us and members of the Muslim Brotherhood.

Then I spoke to my 'beloved' directly. I discovered, feeling extremely jealous, that another student was in love with her and that he had followed her to the female students' housing. I sent her a message containing a lesson in the behavior appropriate to a committed Muslim young woman. She came to me and called me out of dissection class to talk to me, weeping and complaining of the harshness of my message and asking about the logic of imposing part of the responsibility on her. I apologized, trying to lighten the tone of the conversation and deliberately stringing it out, so that it went on for about forty-five minutes. Before that, my highest hope would have been that my eye might just once catch hers.

> Marvel'st thou that
> My longing for a sight of her near slays me
> Yet, at her approach, I avert my gaze?
> Some say tis for my creed and that is true.
> Yet true too it is that
> Ne'er have I faced the sun before
> And not cast down my eyes before its blaze.

I wrote these verses after that encounter, when I found myself no longer able to concentrate on my studies. Just like any other eighteen-year-old, I would spend, in addition to the hours on the telephone with her friend, further hours with a male friend of mine giving vent to my feelings as we wracked our brains together over what I could do. I forgot about the girl to whom I had asked to be betrothed a year before so that I could help to keep myself obedient to God, and was overwhelmed by a new kind of love full of emotions, anxiety, sleeplessness, palpitations of the heart, and poetry. I discovered, however, from my telephone friend that the object of my affections did not share my feelings. She was outstanding academically and her father owned a private hospital, in which she would work as soon as she graduated from medical school. I, on the other hand, had, as she put it, a "special situation" that precluded any long-term commitment between us.

The whole universe was conspiring against me, bursting in on me in the apartment where I spent hours in isolation preparing for the make-up exams. One day, I woke up to an extraordinary piece of news: Saddam Hussein had invaded Kuwait.

The period between the violent confrontations that Asyut had witnessed during the previous academic year and Saddam's invasion of Kuwait had seen a temporary truce between the Jama'a and the regime. We were allowed to hold meetings and to have access to the Rahma Mosque, in place of that of the Jam'iya Shar'iya. The leadership of the Jama'a remained in prison, however, and the atmosphere continued to be tense. Then the invasion came along and stirred up the calm waters. At a single stroke, one that I had never imagined could happen, the whole world, including mine, was thrown into turmoil. At first, we thought the invasion was welcome news, that God was driving the tyrants into confrontation with one another, and that they would "smash their idols with their own hands," as the brothers put it, the idol being smashed in this case being Arab Nationalism. Later, though, the complex nature of what had happened was revealed. We had been right to consider it a mortal blow against our sworn enemies. What we had not reckoned with was that it was, also, a sword that could be used to slay us too, as a group whose project was the establishment of a state based on a comprehensive Islamic order.

Ard al-Islam, the Land of Islam, is every land over which the banner of Islam has flown in the past or flies today, including Spain and parts of China that were wrested from the Muslims by force. This does not, however, mean that either of the latter is an Abode of Islam. That concept belongs to a different system of categorization, one that applies to all the nations of the world, irrespective of whether Islam reached them in the past or whether Muslims are present in them. The Abode of Islam is those countries in which the laws of Islam are enforced, while the Abode of War is those in which they are not enforced. The *takfiri* (anathematizing) Islamist groups, which shun all contact with society, base their thinking on these two categories only. The Jama'a Islamiya, however, adds a third, which is those countries most of whose population are Muslims but whose rulers are unbelievers. This category embraces Egypt and all other Islamic countries with the exception (at that time) of parts of Afghanistan. The theoretical basis for this distinction was laid down by Ibn Taymiya (which accounts for his importance in the eyes of the Islamist movement) when the Mongols invaded and governed Islamic states while their peoples remained Muslims.

Ibn Taymiya was no longer with us and we didn't know what to do in this new, practical test – one unbelieving ruler of a state whose people were Muslims in confrontation with another unbelieving ruler of a state whose people were Muslims. That was the starting point. The riddle got more difficult, however: an alliance of Crusaders and unbelieving regimes ruling Muslim states was preparing to invade a land belonging to Islam headed by an unbelieving regime.

When one reads a difficult bit in a book one can skip it, maybe cursing the writer and accusing him of going on for too long and being boring. The Jama'a Islamiya, however, and indeed the Islamist movement as a whole, did not possess that luxury. They couldn't simply turn a blind eye to those months in the history of the region. They couldn't tell people, "This is a difficult bit, please turn the page, and go on to the next. Oh, you don't know what comes next? In that case, please refer to what we wrote before. You'll find it simple, straightforward, and easy to understand, as well as enjoyable, undemanding, and entertaining."

Some Jama'a statements called for neutrality in a war between tyrants and unbelievers that would deplete the resources of both. But what should be done if the unbelievers won and occupied Iraq? Others called for the defense of a land of Islam, in the form of the Gulf, which was being desecrated by the feet of unbelievers who were preparing to invade another land of Islam, in the form of Iraq. The appeal of this group was enhanced by seductive revolutionary emotions and the possibility of riding the wave of opposition to the war on the street. The Jama'a put on a festival in celebration of the Baathist poet Muhammad Afifi Matar, whom the Egyptian authorities had arrested, and whom the Jama'a had confused with the Iraqi Islamist poet Ahmad Matar. A brother from medical school read out the Iraqi poet's verse. I was amazed that none of the brothers realized, throughout the long period of preparation for this festival of oratory, that the person arrested was an Egyptian Baathist who had nothing in common with us and with whom we had nothing in common. I waited until the end of the festival and then alerted the current leadership to the situation. My awareness of his identity was no stroke of genius on my part; I simply read the one state-owned and one opposition newspaper that we bought at home every morning, and the news was everywhere. On another occasion, Brother Elhami el-Salamuni preached a sermon at the Friday prayer enquiring, "Is it not possible that God may have guided Saddam's heart unawares to us?" During the sermon, with patent and disturbing demagogy, he called on God to "guide Saddam's heart and make him into one of Your warriors," contradicting by so doing the article of the Islamic Action Charter relating to "concurrence," which stipulates that "we concur on one goal, with one creed, under one ideological flag."

I saw my future as being that of a theorist, one who reached his conclusions judiciously, without seeking to please the common people or the mob, and I was totally for the first stance (neutrality), primarily for reasons based on the shari'a, but for strategic reasons too. This position was preferable in the long term, I believed, because it sowed resentment among the ranks of the common people, tarnished the gloss of the Arab Nationalist concept, and undermined the legitimacy of the Arab regimes. We had not, for example, made war on Israel and would never waste our effort on fighting it until we had brought down the regime in Egypt. This was because "fighting the regime has a higher priority than fighting the unbelievers" and because it was the nearer enemy from whom we could never feel safe if it was to be at our backs when we fought the more distant enemy. Despite this, I listened to Iraqi radio and was admiring of its revolutionary rhetoric. I would memorize words that I had never heard before, such as 'Indochina,' 'Bay of Pigs,' and 'Che Guevara' (I couldn't pronounce 'Ho Chi Minh'), just as I used to memorize the terms used by Freud without understanding what they meant.

This was the first time I had formulated a critique of the Jamaʿa, perhaps because its real leadership was absent and in their absence I dreamed of a role for myself; in addition, I loved intellectual contrariness, which, in their absence, I found an opportunity to express. Quite simply, I felt that the crystal goblet of pure Islam, which had been shattered following the Prophet's death, was still in pieces, and that each party had picked up a single piece of it, into which it gazed, only to find the reflection of its own wishes, which it then trumpeted in the name of Islam. I did not, however, attribute these shortcomings to the ideas of the Islamist movement but rather to their deflection, under the seductiveness of specific circumstances and in the absence of its experienced leadership, from the pure and undiluted origins of Islamic thought. When the Great Islamic Schism occurred between Ali ibn Abi Talib and Muʿawiya, and the two opponents agreed on arbitration to be carried out by two delegations of their wise men in order to put an end to the fighting, Ali told his delegation, "Do not debate with them over the Qur'an, for it wears many faces." Were things any different now? Would they be tomorrow?

When I told Sheikh Saʿd of my criticisms, he told me that the security services had sent a message to the brothers enquiring as to their position on the war in the light of Sheikh Elhami's sermon, and that the Jamaʿa had responded indirectly that the latter constituted a personal opinion of Sheikh Elhami's and not the position of the Jamaʿa. Things remained calm. Indeed, there was even greater relaxation of the government's grip, since the latter, with its participation in the coalition forces, was anxious to avoid stirring up the street. There was also some relief for me on a personal level when I passed the make-up exams and was thus able to continue with the second year of medical school. In this I was helped by senior brothers, whose duties, onerous at that time, did not prevent them from setting aside some time to explain to me the lessons I found difficult. My new academic year also started in this period of calm, and was the only year at the University of Asyut in which I was able to sit the midyear exams.

Clichés often lie but also often speak the truth. In any case, this really was "the calm before the storm."

Sheikh Tal'at Yasin was sitting on the steps of the Rahma Mosque, his arms embracing his knees, his head was resting on the latter, and his face entirely hidden, looking into the depths of the human abyss. Despite this, it was clear from the shaking of his shoulders and his sobs, audible to anyone who went past him, that he was weeping. Sheikh Tal'at Yasin was one of those people who radiate charisma. Everything about him was different. His style of preaching seemed wonderful if you were watching him but insupportable if you could only hear him. He was short, of fair complexion, and moved, when standing in front of a row of worshipers to lead them in prayer, in a way that reminded one of a character in a children's puppet play, his fingers intertwined, the palms parallel to the ground and facing downward, and his arms stretched out. He moved his legs with a distinctive rhythm, bending his body with every step – a spontaneous choreography of the simplest sort. On his own he would prepare half the posters for the university's wall magazine exhibitions, writing out the captions, choosing the pictures and arranging them, and he would directly supervise the other half, tasks that would keep him up for two days in a row, while on the third he would sleep only in snatches. He had been the youngest of the Brothers of '81 to memorize the Qur'an in prison, being then only eighteen years old. Once I saw him kiss Sheikh Abd el-Akher Hammad on his forehead in celebration of his release from prison, an eccentric gesture that only someone as instinctively affectionate and creative as Sheikh Tal'at Yasin would have thought of. Only those who were close to him could appreciate this affectionateness, according to those who were close to him, and I had not been afforded that chance to any real degree. Two years before, he had taught us how to write statements, or leaflets, at the proselytization school, and then given us a test, in which it was my luck to get seven out of ten, the highest mark among that group of students. His introverted nature (despite this engineering student being the Jama'a's amir at the university), his liking for solitude, writing, reading, and creativity, and, above all, the rareness of his words, which emerged from his mouth one by one, as though being born one after the other, all helped to explain why he had few friends. One of those few was Ala' Muhyi el-Din, a comrade of his in prison and his friend in the years after their release.

What happened to Ala' that day was out of keeping with the calm of the preceding year. The air strikes on Iraq did not begin until the middle of the academic year and the ground war didn't begin until later in the second term. I took the end-of-year exam and did well in all second-year subjects as well as in the ones I'd carried over from the year before. Throughout this period, the regime was careful not to provoke us, especially as we were not the most prominent opponents of the war. This lack of provocation created a tense calm like that which binds the hostage to his captor, or a penitent to his beloved sin. Because the brothers who had been arrested before the war remained in prison, the vacuum brought me, for a period, into close contact with myself, in a world without mirrors, it being said in a Hadith of the Prophet that "the believer is a mirror unto his brother." Brother Majed, who had recently arrived from Sohaj, the governorate to which I belonged by origin and birth though not by residence, had a wonderful voice when he recited the Qur'an. He was polite, quiet-spoken, and brave. When he had been arrested the summer before, he had managed to strike out at the two soldiers who were guarding him in the car, and escape. He didn't tell me this but I discovered it from the brothers.

On one occasion he heard me telling, as I often did at that time, jokes that contained sexual innuendos, albeit quite innocent ones. I was higher than him in the organization's hierarchy, or so at least I thought, but he took me aside and told me sternly, "It's not right for you to be a representative of the Jama'a to the students and talk like that." He rarely made jokes, uttered all the various devotions due at various times of the day, and never missed the dawn prayer. I responded to his advice with something to the effect that merriment, in all its forms, was present throughout history and that this was the way I was. I may have said this merely out of obstinacy, or perhaps because I really couldn't change myself. The rare mirror did not reflect a pleasing picture.

The level of public prosetylization during this period of vacuum was not really much better than my personal level of conduct. In reality, the Jama'a kept a low profile, undertaking activities such as printing the aides-mémoire that collected for the students the questions from the previous years' exams. Even this was a difficult task. The security apparatus kept printers under tight control, and they would as a result refuse to print anything bearing the name of the Jama'a. This put us in an embarrassing position, as the students paid for these aides-mémoire in advance and the midyear exams were almost upon us. I decided not to wait, but to print an alternative that consisted of an identical copy, minus the logo of the Jama'a and any other reference to it. When it reached the brother in charge that I had decided to do this, he reacted strongly, especially given that he had paid already a cash advance to have them printed, and from his own pocket. Despite his objections, I went ahead with my decision once the deadline that I'd set him to find a press that would print them with the Jama'a's logo had passed. He told me, as though repeating a fact we were both agreed on, "You're rebellious." This was the third occasion on which one of my direct superiors had described me as having this characteristic, one that was not acceptable in times of crisis when the Jama'a needed self-abnegating foot soldiers; and when the characterization came from Brother Yaser Fathi, it had a special significance. First, he was the leading brother who, despite his important responsibilities, had carved out the time to help explain to me the lessons that I hadn't been able to grasp at medical school. Second, he was executed shortly thereafter, and the words of martyrs have a special quality – as with martyrdom itself, they both deliver a deadly blow and restore life. Yaser was not the only person I knew to meet with martyrdom. Before him there was Mahmud, the youth who was sent at the end of the eighties, when he was seventeen, to Afghanistan and was killed there. Mahmud, however, was a special case. Yaser's martyrdom, though, was part of a chain of events, a chain that began that day, the day that Ala' Muhyi el-Din was assassinated.

The assassination of the official spokesman of the Jama'a, following this year of calm, was a message from the Egyptian authorities that could be understood by anyone who could read. The regime, supported, following its role in the Gulf War, by the New World Order, would not tolerate any activity by the Jama'a, be it peaceful or violent. Ala' Muhyi el-Din was the link between the Jama'a, the media, and other institutions, and even with certain state apparatuses that needed from time to time to talk to someone who could speak for the Jama'a with confidence. Such a media interface would be, according to the basic rules of armed struggle, at the furthest possible distance from any underground structure. The assassination was, therefore, a herald of the inevitable confrontation between our group, which believed in jihad as the sole means in the end to change a regime that did not maintain God's laws, and a state that did not permit even peaceful, much less violent, opposition.

Tal'at Yasin gave warning of the approaching storm in the words he uttered as he stood on the steps, wiping away his tears: "Ala's blood will not be shed for nothing." When Tal'at Yasin subsequently went into hiding, the whole world changed. He was the last of the leaders whose vision counted for something important in and of itself. Day after day, we proceeded like a company that has changed the nature of its enterprise, relinquishing its activities in a certain sector but wanting to retain a small number of workers in order to sell off the old stock. There were no prominent proselytizers left and no prominent writers. One day, the brothers were at a loss as to how to write the statement giving the Jama'a's position on the events of the week that was to be issued, as was usual, at the Monday meeting. They therefore set a group of individuals the task of writing separate statements, out of which they chose mine, which was entitled "The Egyptian Government and the Nazarene Campaign" – a choice that would never have been made before, short of the Jamaʿa being stricken by a plague; and indeed what had befallen the Jamaʿa was nothing less than a plague – one that had carried off the horses and spared the lame donkey.

During that summer vacation, I started feeling as though I was in a stifling prison. I left the house rarely, and my activities were restricted. In one of those unconsidered moments that can bring about critical change, I decided to transfer my papers from the College of Medicine, University of Asyut, to the College of Medicine, Cairo University, but my father refused to agree. Perhaps he thought that this would deprive the family of the least that they could hope for, which was that I should be under their eye. He was unaware that at that unreflective moment, I wanted, in the depths of my soul, to be liberated and that I was feeling that Asyut, with its limited horizons and its restricted activities, indeed, even with the brothers whom I knew and who knew me, in the supervisory sense of that word, had become a prison to me.

I know that this must seem a strange way for a committed group member such as myself to have thought, but it was not really so. These are moments of weakness that happen to everyone, but which in my case were part of my permanent crisis with myself, which created within me a feeling that my heart was not one hundred percent at ease, and that I could never therefore hope to be a truly committed Muslim or believer. A very complex thing emotionally, with a path as complicated as the biological path by which a sip of juice moves from place to place in the body: we may be able to trace it anatomically, but we can't easily define its physiological influences on our vital functions. Even more difficult to define is the histological impact of this same sip on each cell and tissue of this same sip. What then are we to do with millions of sips, in the form of ideas, beliefs, and behaviors? I knew the path down which I was proceeding, and I knew the goal that I had to reach by traveling it, namely that God should be satisfied with me.

The problem lay in how God's satisfaction, or its outward manifestation, was to be apprehended. The unknown future is a vast terrain for the interpretation of such manifestations. My family's objections to the transfer of my papers to Cairo University must be a matter of destiny. God did not wish me to leave; He did not wish me to flee my destiny. Earlier, when I first became a committed Muslim, Sheikh Usama had advised me not to spend the summer vacation in Cairo, and I had gone against his wishes and he had proved to be right. The road was still long, and I could see on it nothing of His manifestations, which I had come to know well from the stories of the earliest Muslims. I had yet to be afflicted in my wealth, my health, or my soul, and this exemption from affliction meant that there was still far to go. After all those years with the Jama'a, I still had the vague idea that the individual's obedience to God was a mutual, cosmic understanding, a dialogue between the worshiper and the worshiped, which for me was summed up by the Hadith Qudsi which says, "He who approaches Me by a hand's span, I shall approach by a cubit, and he who approaches Me by a cubit, I shall approach by an arm's length, and he who comes to Me walking, I shall come to him running."

"Why, though, O Lord, in running toward us do You visit afflictions on what we love? Why cannot Your running toward us be purely luminous, like that of the angels?"

Alif lam mim. Do the people reckon that they will be left to say "We believe" and they will not be tried? We certainly tried those that were before them, and assuredly God knows those who speak truly, and assuredly He knows the liars (Qur'an 29:3).

"Even the separate letters alif lam mim, with which this chapter of the Qur'an opens, make up, when joined, the word *alam*, or pain. Can there be faith without pain?"

If you believe in God totally, and you believe that Paradise is for the believers, then why, in God's name, would not any idiot in the world cut short this life, with all its hardship and adversity, and go to Paradise, with all its ease? We cannot, however, do without this world. I, at least, could not do without this world. Did this not mean, quite simply, that a part of me did not believe in the next? It must be so, I would say to myself in frank heresy, after which I would spit three times to my left, this being the prophetically approved behavior should Satan send ideas into the mind of a believer designed to seduce him. "Can you explain why I don't weep when I hear the Qur'an, and weep when I hear stories of lover's partings and meetings?" I asked the brother called 'el-Nubi,' who was much given to weeping, at least according to the brothers' descriptions of him, as I walked with him one night. "It means that your heart is tender, which is a sign of faith," replied the brother, but his reply did not satisfy me. The reply that satisfied me I would find in another weeping, one of a different sort.

An acquaintance of mine, who lived on the same street as the Rahma Mosque, had changed to a startling degree recently. Only a few months before, he would come to the prayer with us from time to time, and his mother and father, who were both professors at the College of Pharmacology, were religiously observant, even though they had no connection to the Jama'a Islamiya. Suddenly, this young man started fasting every day and when he came to the prayer, he had only to hear the Qur'an to start weeping loudly, on one note, like a long cry of pain. I felt that the sound was sincere and contained a suppressed complaint and I felt that it contained something that I lacked. I wanted that sound. I wanted it to come out of me, for if it did so, it would relieve me of many things. Firstly, it would release me from the prison of the body, would make me conquer that enemy forever and direct at it a final, mortal blow that would make it into a warrior on my behalf, just as the martyred brothers and the brothers of great courage had done. These had all succeeded in conquering their bodies, taming them, and subjecting them to their will. I would never be able to join their ranks if I were not victorious in that battle first. The prevailing vacuum was a suitable opportunity to enter the battle. For the first time since joining the Jama'a, I bought works by the Sufi Abu Hamid al-Ghazali. For the first time I took care to utter all the various devotions due before the sunset prayer and after the dawn prayer, just as I had previously been keen to read a new book or compose a sermon. I also took to getting up regularly at night to pray. I prayed the dawn prayer forty days consecutively without interruption (Satan had stopped urinating in my ear). I stopped watching half-naked women on television, even when I was alone in the house. Before, that had been a temptation I was incapable of resisting; I would do whatever it took to steal a few minutes contemplating Sophia Loren's amazing bust in *Two Women* or Claudia Cardinale's back as she removed her nightdress in front of her kidnapper in some Western. During the 1991 Iraq War, when I brought a television into my room, I'd interrupt the news in order to watch a movie.

✳

Maybe because of the absence of first-class orators, maybe because I showed more enthusiasm and concentration, maybe because I was then at peace with the fact that this was my life, I progressed massively with regard to public speaking. I became more relaxed and much less sensational. I was able to tackle broader issues and, more importantly, to improvise, to make jokes, and to speak in a low voice whenever I wanted, without fear that people's attention might wander. Moreover, brothers dispatched me to important mosques outside Asyut, such as those of Manfalut and Tema, where I discovered that I could conquer my nerves in tense security conditions. I knew the security risks but I kept on doing my duty all the same.

There was another factor that helped push me toward this change. That summer vacation I completed my memorization of the Qur'an and, at the same time, my reading of the six volumes of Sayyid Qutb's magnificent book *Fi zilal al-Qur'an* (In the Shadow of the Qur'an), as well as Mahmud Shaker's *Tarikh al-Islam* (The History of Islam). To complete the Qur'an is a great honor, and a greater responsibility. It was as though the Prophet (pbuh) had placed something in my hand, then closed my hand and patted it. For three days I did nothing but pray and then read from *al-Rahiq al-makhtum* (The Sealed Nectar) on the life of the Prophet. After one dawn prayer, I came to the end of the book and my eyes filled with tears in a way that I had never felt before. I felt a lightness I had never before experienced. For the first time in my life I felt that I was pure, pure as though there were no shit in my intestines, as though there were a distance between me and my body, as though I would see only what I wanted to see and hear only what I had first filtered of all impurity, as though ... .

In a dream, I saw myself praying, and I interpreted the dream, as I had been taught, with a verse from the Qur'an.

✳

It was the first week of my third year in college. The previous day had been a holiday, in honor of the Sixth of October War, and today I would return to my routine. Following the advice of one of my colleagues, who was making top grades, I woke up early – which I did naturally because of the dawn prayer – and read through the lessons that the professor would be covering that day. This would transform what the professor said into a second reading that would help crystallize the topic rather than lead to wasted time, as it would do if one listened to a lecture whose vocabulary and orientation were completely unfamiliar. I wanted to pass with honors that year. I would abandon my desk facing the wall and study at a folding table that I would set up in front of the balcony, with a glass of strong tea. On this particular day, I didn't dawdle but at 7.30 exactly left what remained of the tea in the glass and hurried to campus. I greeted my uncle on my mother's side, who was a police officer now working as a university security guard. In fact, I tried to avoid him but he greeted me first, and even introduced me to his colleague, telling him that my mother was his aunt's daughter. I didn't want to embarrass him, especially on that day.

The brothers had decided to change the equation of tense calm at the University of Asyut, and had asked us to assemble in the morning, then distribute ourselves among the university's amphitheaters and deliver simultaneous sermons. I had learned of this the day before and one of the brothers had passed on to me that I would be responsible for this demarche. I was delighted; I believed that I now deserved such a mission. I found the brothers assembled together as agreed but discovered Brother Umar addressing them as though he were in charge. It transpired that there were two groups of leaders outside of the university, who were working without coordination, and that there had been some confusion. Since it had been decided that my role would be to lead the action, and I did not have a role as a speechmaker, I ended up with no role at all, apart from entering the amphitheater in which another brother would speak and sitting with the rest of the students. I observed suspicious activity among the security informants, who were going in and out of the amphitheaters searching for individuals. When I left and went down into the main courtyard of the university, it was clear from the heavy presence of informants and officers of the university security force that something was afoot. Then I received a message from the brothers that I should try to escape, because I was on the wanted list and security was looking for me.

I don't know why I didn't take the matter seriously even then, though perhaps that is not the best way to put it. It was more that I couldn't believe in the depths of my soul that such a thing could happen. I believed, for some reason, that I was at the bottom of the list: if they found me in front of them, they would arrest me; if not, they wouldn't expend any great effort to do so. I also felt that, even if I had come to merit arrest, this wouldn't happen for some time. That sensation of inner lightness had occurred only a week ago, and I had seen the dream only a week ago, so it was impossible that God would speed up the process in this way, with this cruelty. However that might be, I sketched out to myself a plan of escape. I moved with my fellow students to another building, the one where we took practical classes. I agreed with the teaching assistant, who was sympathetic to the Jama'a, that I should leave with the other students at the end of the class and under the eyes of the plainclothes security men, lead them down all together on the ground floor and then go back quickly and enter the classroom before they could notice. He would then lock the classroom door on me. This plan depended, of course, on my speed and physical fitness as a soccer player.

I left the classroom with the other students, hanging back so that I would be among the last, then pushed in front of the others as I went down to the ground floor, making sure that each informer on each floor got a good look at me. As soon as I reached the bottom, I strolled about here and there as though looking for a way out. The informers assembled in readiness to arrest me as soon as I should leave the building. However, I didn't leave but went to the 'up' staircase, then made a sign to them with two fingers and the whistling sound we use in Egypt to summon a dog. I knew that they wouldn't follow me directly if I signaled to them in this insulting way. I walked up the first flight of steps slowly, looking at them and making the same gestures, and as soon as I turned onto the second flight and disappeared from their sight, I started running as fast as I could to the third floor, where the classroom was. The teaching assistant was waiting for me at the door and I went in and he locked the door from the outside as he would normally do and left as though everything was normal. Listening from inside the classroom, I heard the muffled sounds of the security men as they called questions to one another and the sound of their footsteps and their shouts to the people in the lavatories to come out.

I stayed in that classroom for three to four hours. The sounds died away completely and the day was drawing to a close. The teaching assistant came back and unlocked the door and told me that a brother would be waiting for me on a motorcycle if I climbed over the wall that gave onto the highway. I was uncomfortable with this plan, though. I preferred to escape on foot, firstly because I had not previously tested how difficult the wall might be to climb, critical given the short time I would have in which to do so, and secondly because the possible consequences of escaping on a motorcycle, if the police opened fire on us or even if we had an accident as a result of the pursuit, were very frightening.

I set off, walking fast but not running, in the direction of the university's side gate, which was next to the teaching faculty housing. I'd thought I would enter one of the housing blocks as this was my most logical escape route. I knew their entrances and exits and the places where one could hide there very well, and I might be able to get away in the car of one of my friends who lived there. I also believed that the security forces would think very hard before arresting me inside. Then I remembered the scene in which I had left the housing in tears eight years before and decided that I wouldn't go in there or ask the help of anyone from there, however bad things might be. In any case, I was now only a few steps from the gate.

"Mr. al-Berry!" called a voice. Not far behind me was a police car and men with sticks and revolvers were leaping out of it. I stopped and surrendered to my fate. My dream had turned out to be true, and in accordance with the verse that I had used to interpret it: *Them you shall detain after the prayer, and they shall swear by God .... Our testimony is truer than their testimony* (Qur'an 5:106) (God has spoken truly).

4

Temptation

Egyptian movies love to poke fun at well-dressed persons who find themselves in the police lockup along with drug dealers and criminals, the scene usually ending with the well-dressed person receiving a stinging slap on the face and then screaming for help from the sergeant on guard by the cell. In the police car, I was overcome by an unusual calm and all I could think of was the aforementioned scene. I wanted to laugh but didn't know why. I entered the cell with three or four from the Jama'a arrested the same day and there were others there who'd been arrested on charges of selling hashish. One of them informed us that he was the son of the mortuary worker at our college, so I felt reassured. These people were extremely quiet and occupied one corner of the cell, while we sat in another.

On the evening of the second day, we were transferred to the public prosecution building, where we sat in front of the prosecutor's office under guard of two officers, waiting our turn to be interrogated, while the place was surrounded by Central Security troops and armed policemen. I let my eyes roam, seeking a means of escape, not because I wanted to, but because it is a religious duty to make every effort to escape from captivity. I made my assessment mechanically, knowing that it would end with my choosing not to flee, since, should I do so, I would have to live somewhere other than in our house and I would never, no matter how much time passed, be able to go back to the university. One of the officers chatted with us while the other showed his disgust and looked at us suspiciously. The first said he was sure we loved Egypt and acted as we did in the belief that this was in her interest. Then he asked the oldest of the brothers, "Go on. Tell me the truth. Don't you love Egypt?" to which the brother replied, "Of course I love Egypt. That's why I want her to return to being 'God's quiver on earth.'" The officer spoke of the importance of internal security and stability, so that Egypt could be strong and the brother spoke of the importance of its being under Islamic rule, so that it could get rid of corruption and be strong. The disgusted officer remained as he was and said nothing, the palm of his right hand resting on the back of his left, the two of them resting on the curve of his belly while he passed the time glowering at what he heard, glancing around in an attempt to avoid looking at the speakers, and puffing and blowing, puffing and blowing.

When it was my turn to go in and see the prosecutor, my nerves were calm. I entered the room shackled to the wrist of a policeman, which caused the prosecutor to yell at the officer in protest at this open breach of procedure. The officer apologized to the prosecutor, took me outside, and undid my handcuffs. This made me feel yet more at ease. When I entered the room again, I discovered in the light that there was a lot of dust on my pants, so I brushed it off. This time it was my turn to be yelled at by the prosecutor: "Do you think you're in a cloakroom here?" The lawyer who was with us apologized, looking at me reproachfully. My interrogation turned on my speechmaking and rabble-rousing at the college, and on my directing criticisms at the regime and at the person of Mrs. Suzanne Mubarak. This wasn't true: I hadn't made a single speech at the college that day and it was all trumped-up charges, which is what I said. It seems that the prosecutor believed me, for he gave the order for my release. As I left the interrogation, I found my father and cousin waiting. My father gave me a blanket and some clothes, held my hand, and said, "Don't worry. Be a man, and keep your spirits up."

Following the prosecutor's decision, the security authorities – whom in Egypt we refer to as 'the government' – had two options, to which there was no third: either to carry out the order for my release, or to detain me without trial under the Emergency Law, which would entail transferring me to a prison in Cairo. In the event, it did choose a third option – a surprise option that the State Security authorities had added to the list, namely, of transferring us to the security barracks in Asyut, which was a military installation, where the law forbade the holding of civilians.

Despite the exceedingly bad reputation of the place, it allowed me to cling to some degree of hope that we would not be detained long and that the security forces would wait until the three or four days for which the prosecutor had directed that some of us should be detained for questioning had passed and then release us all at one go.

✳

From the moment that I was placed in that Godforsaken place, far from any human habitation, I understood the meaning of the word 'prison.' For the first three days, it was just Majed and me, in a cell not more than four meters square, with a height of about five meters. In the wall was a small window with three iron bars, which we couldn't reach even standing on the other's shoulders. We ate the same food as the police privates – in the early morning huge stewed beans, and in the middle of the day rice, meat, and vegetables. I expressed my wonder at the quantity of food only for my companion to give me the good tidings that, "They feed you up by day so that you can stand what they're going to do to you by night." In any case, I didn't have an appetite, and Majed delivered the ruling that the meat and everything cooked in its broth was forbidden by religion because it was imported; thus we ended up surviving on the beans alone. Later, he assured me that the old cooking-fat can in which they gave us our drinking water was the very same that was placed in the privates' bathroom for them to use to clean themselves with after defecating and urinating. He was quite certain of this, so I stopped drinking water too.

Night in the cell, which begins two hours before the sunset prayer, is pitch black. No other night is like it. The only thing that disturbs it is the grating of iron on iron as the bolts of other cells are opened, summoning new detainees to interrogation. It was our bad luck that a problem had arisen at that time between the security forces and the inhabitants of a village falling within Asyut's administrative area, with the result that the number of those held was large and the screaming almost never ceased due to the beatings. Majed used the daylight to read the Qur'an, saying we had plenty of time to talk at night. It is a sign of piety that one should desire the company of God more than that of men; if he had responded to my attempts at conversation and not set a limit to them, the time would have passed in idle talk. I didn't greatly enjoy talking at night. I missed that certain feeling that emanates from the expressions on the face of the other, from the looks in his eyes; even so, I would have liked to prolong such conversations. Majed wouldn't let me talk for long, but would ask me to join him in prayer in the darkness, for such prayers are never refused, or would ask me to review with him the parts of the Qur'an we had memorized. The first night, I recited from memory six continuous *rub*'s from the chapter of *al-Baqara* (The Cow) in the Qur'an. He was amazed when he found out that I'd learned the whole Qur'an by heart, and that I'd done so just in the few years with the Jama'a. He himself had not even then yet learned the Qur'an by heart, even though he had been detained before, such periods generally providing the best opportunity. The following day, when new detainees of our group came to join us in our cell, we had something new to keep us occupied – waiting for each person as he returned from interrogation in order to ask him what had happened to him, and what information he had given away.

Two brothers – Esam, a young man from a village near Asyut whom I'd met for the first time twenty-four hours earlier, and Majed, the exemplary brother – had preceded me to the interrogation room. Both were tortured with electricity. I heard each voice let out a short scream followed, after a brief silence, by a long, quavering scream. I didn't know the dimensions of the place I was in. It didn't mean anything that I could hear the screams of those being tortured; even in the cell, I'd been able to hear their voices – they were far off and had a multiple echo, but were audible. Now, however, I realized that, even though I was in the truck, I was very close. I could hear one of the two voices saying, "I give in, sir. I'll tell you everything." When, however, its owner, after catching his breath, continued to refuse to speak, the scream would rise again.

I was blindfolded, sitting in the truck, not knowing whether there were others with me or not. Around me I could hear whispers that I couldn't make out; there might be brothers I didn't know with me, or perhaps guards, or goons, I couldn't tell. All I could think about was what was going to happen to me. Would I be tortured like them? Would I be able to hold out? How should I address the officer? Should I call him 'sir'? It was a word I'd never used, and it stuck in my throat. In the end, though, it was just an insignificant detail; the brother who had used it to the officer hadn't revealed a single piece of information, and that was what mattered. Anyway, my desire not to use it wasn't born of courage, but of a pride that could be broken with a slap.

I waited for a very long time. It would have been better if they'd started with me. I turned into two separate beings; this is not a figure of speech but the truth. Part of me, whose exact nature I could not specify, would go to the interrogation room and return to my blindfolded body with the scene in minute detail – the color of the gray undershirt worn by the brother who was being interrogated, the white face of the officer and his reddish-brown mustache, the gray paint of the walls and the sweating damp spots in a corner of the ceiling and all the way along the wall opposite the door; the four privates wearing dirty beige Central Security uniforms who led the brother inside, and the goons who stood next to him and carried out the beating or electrocution, according to the officer's rapid, abbreviated gestures, one of them wearing a jallabiya and a gray skullcap, the other a similar jallabiya and a dark green skullcap. My body shrank into itself with physically illogical speed, and I felt that I'd become a mere gecko on the mesh window of the truck, that I could leave if I wanted, could go out and release myself from what was coming to me. It was up to me, and all I had to do was take a decision. It was a seductive idea to be a gecko at that moment, but I had to think of what the consequences would be some hours from now, when I had to look at my cellmates and find them still humans. It was difficult for me to take that particular decision, so I took two others instead. One was that after this night I would never again be scared of the oral exams at college; the professor who was examining you might look at you in disgust, or humiliate you with a word, or fail to give you a passing grade, but he would never take a whip out of the drawer of his desk and hit you with it, or deliberately put your hand into the electricity socket. The second decision concerned a family matter.

Then it was my turn. I wondered what I would have to say to them when I returned to the cell. It was the first time I had faced a State Security interrogation. Would this be used in my defense if I was weak? I was not ordinarily a weak person, or at least so I thought, though even my need to talk to other people while in the cell was something I hadn't known about myself before. I could maintain a wall of silence with my family for long periods, during which none of them would dare challenge me. The favorite punishment at home, especially from my mother, was to stop addressing any conversation to the person being punished. The first time I was subjected to this, I begged my mother and sister to talk to me and they refused. My mother told my father, as she put the dirty clothes in the washing machine, "He did such and such. Let him learn some manners." After this, I took pride in being obstinate, like Taha Hussein (as I put it) and in not being the first to talk no matter what happened. In truth, if there were an international championship for not speaking to people, I'd be among the top-ranked players. I would refuse to speak to my mother, or my sister, for three months, limiting myself to saying, if I wanted something, "Ahmad (the name of my younger brother), tell her such and such." Once when my father slapped me in front of my colleagues, I stopped talking to him for six months, no matter how hard he tried to engage me in conversation. All this was before I joined the Jama'a. And even then, although the rules of Islam do not permit anyone to refuse to speak to someone else for more than three days, I made an exception for my family. Now, as I waited for the interrogation, I realized that this was a trivial matter compared to the situation I was in. That second decision that I took was never to do so again.

They pushed me into the interrogation room, my eyes blindfolded, my hands handcuffed. The room was very close; after they'd taken me down out of the truck I didn't have to go more than four or five steps before the feeling of my surroundings changed, from the open air, where I could feel a breath of wind, to an almost enclosed space where I could hear the echo of my footsteps and the rustle of my clothes and of those who were leading me. "Take his handcuffs off," the officer said. "I know he'll talk right away, now that he's heard the one before him." Then, directing his words to me, he said, "The one before you tried to play the hero and not say anything, so I made him talk using my own special methods, and I got six pages out of him, so you'd better talk right away." Immediately I said, "Of course. I'll tell you anything I know." He asked me the usual questions about my civil status and whether I'd been arrested before, and then he asked the usual questions about the Jama'a's leaders in the different sectors, and I told him the names we'd agreed upon beforehand with the brothers, which were all names of people who were in prison, or of known brothers the mention of whom would do no harm. He didn't accuse me of lying, since the brothers who had gone before me would certainly have told him the same names. Nevertheless, he disputed the one name that I was sure of, 'Ahmad Abduh Salim,' amir of the Jama'a Islamiya in Asyut. He told me my information was out of date and the brothers had changed their amir in Asyut and chosen Sheikh Murtada in place of Salim: "So your amir's a man with a vocational diploma, and you're at medical school." The interrogation went off without incident and I emerged, unable to believe myself.

In the cell, I went over what the questioning had yielded with my two companions. Majed was surprised that the interrogator had known about "the day of bonding." I myself didn't know what the "day of bonding" was, and he told me that it was a day when certain selected brothers met together to pray through the night and recite the Qur'an until the dawn prayer. They did this in order to school the instincts in patience and endurance in preparation for carrying out jihad for God's cause. I asked him if he had taken part in such a day himself, and he answered modestly, "Yes." I asked him if he knew that the leader of the Jama'a Islamiya in Asyut was no longer Sheikh Ahmad Abduh Salim, and he said he did. "Two blows to the head hurt," as the proverb says: the brothers had given me some missions, such as being responsible for the brothers in Secondary school, and then for my cohort at college. When it came to serious matters, though, it was as though I wasn't there. I was totally ignorant even of such an important piece of information, which showed their lack of trust in me. Likewise, security hadn't beaten me or tortured me with electricity, as though they too had decided that I was an insignificant being. Majed told me that the moment they uncuffed his hands, as they did mine, he'd pulled the blindfold off his face and punched one of the privates, and I hadn't even thought of doing that. I thought of a sentence on the cover of a *Lucky Luke* adventure book, about coming from a faraway place to a strange land.

The following day, while I was on my way back from the hour outside the cell that they allowed one in order to wash one's face, a thin policeman about fifty years old and with only two stars on his shoulders, meaning that he had risen from the rank of private to that of non-commissioned officer, walked alongside me. He was the one responsible for our cell. He put his hand on my shoulder as we walked along and asked after my well-being and whether I was comfortable or in need of anything. The brothers had told stories of sympathetic jailers whom God had provided of His generosity to make things easier for the oppressed, as well as to provide through them example for the hardhearted, who volunteered to hurt people even when this was not demanded of them. I was in pressing need for this pat on the shoulder; I wanted to tell him that it was precisely what I needed, and to thank him. As we drew close to the cell, and without changing the position of his hand, his fingers took hold of some of the muscles that extend from the neck to the shoulder and he tightened them violently, forcing me to yell and go down on my knees as he insulted me, saying, "You son of a bitch!" Looking at me threateningly and pressing on the same muscle as hard as he could, he then repeated, "You son of a bitch!" He was taking deep breaths and letting them out slowly, and the muscles at the corners of his lips were pulled back, revealing his teeth, as though he were using them to yank a nail from a piece of wood.

The stories of those who have undergone the prison experience are like the memories of a fight that took place in one's adolescence over someone harassing the neighbors' daughter – just funny stories. But the experience itself is different. Prison is a cage in which a person who has complete power imprisons another who has no protection and deprives him of the sight of the sun, of walking in the open air, of going to the toilet, or of seeing friends. He also deprives him of wearing the clothes he chooses and of eating the food he likes. Prison likewise deprives one of his control over time and place. Sometimes it's like a fly that gets into your ear, or a bad headache that won't let you lead a normal life. It's a form of living outside of life. The security camps were close to the Nile. I'd look at the river and think seriously of throwing myself into its waters to escape my feelings of defeat, weakness, and disgrace. I'd look at the palm trees on the bank and cry, remembering my father who used to buy me dates from the market at Tema every Wednesday, even when I wasn't on good terms with him.

Two days after the interrogation, they took us out of the cells and blindfolded us. This time it was during the day, which was suspicious and raised various possibilities, all of them bad. It could be that they were transferring us to State Security to torture us there, where there was no difference between night and day. Or it might be that they had decided to move us to Luman Tura prison, in Cairo, which would put an end to my hope of leaving this hideous place and going straight home. As usual, the surprises thought up by the security forces had no end. As usual, the truck that was carrying us went round in circles, after which we got out and, unusually, the blindfolds were removed from our eyes in front of an office that gave no indication of being a State Security interrogation office. It was like a modest, single-story house in fact, such as one made for the guard of a villa or a gardener in charge of a nursery. The officer ordered us to go down on our knees and place our hands behind our necks. I thought this would be a 'reception party,' when new residents are ordered to pass between two rows of soldiers who hit them randomly with sticks. We stayed in this position for some time. Then an officer ordered me to enter a room. At the door, he ordered me to remove my shoes and socks and stand barefoot. On a chair next to a desk sat a man with a pen in his hand and a large ledger open in front of him. The officer ordered me to kneel again and put my hands behind my neck.

Then the man at the desk started asking me questions about my role in stirring up the students the day I was arrested, as well as incitement to violence and hatred toward the regime. I denied all these charges. When we finished, the man informed me that he was the Legal Affairs officer of the university and that what I had just undergone was the university's disciplinary hearing.

The same day I was taken for another interrogation, at night. This time there was a thin youth with me who had arrived in the cell the same day. The youth was taken into the interrogation room and I was left on my own in the truck blindfolded. The night was completely quiet. The villagers, whom the security forces interrogated every day in their dozens, had departed. The thin boy wasn't a member of the Jama'a; he was just a sympathizer who would go to the mosque from time to time. Despite this, what I was hearing couldn't be anything else. There was no other possible explanation: no sooner did the moaning stop than the screams of electrocution started. When the screaming stopped, I was terror-struck, maybe because of the quiet, or maybe because of black thoughts about people dying under torture, especially someone as weakly built as he; or maybe because the end of the screaming meant that it would soon be my turn. This time there could be no doubt that I'd get what was coming to me. Perhaps they'd reviewed their files and found out who I was, knew every minor and major sin I'd committed, starting with the transportation of leaflets on my bike and ending with leading the brothers in the Secondary schools and making speeches at the university. Indeed, during the last few months I had also been sent to make speeches in towns outside Asyut, such as Tema, Dayrut, and Manfalut. Perhaps my name had been mentioned by mistake by a brother who thought I was already well known to them. If not, then why had they brought just me, along with this young man? They hadn't brought Majed, who had punched the private and seen the officer with his own eyes, and they hadn't brought Esam, who had told us that they'd hung him up with his wrists tied behind his back, the way they did with the dangerous brothers. There had to be some explanation.

The fear I felt was enough to make me do something stupid. I loosened the blindfold and took a quick look through the narrow

opening in the side of the police truck. The entrance to the building was two steps from the opening, and I could see the young
man five meters from the entrance. He wasn't dead or even uncon-
scious. The worst thing is that one remains alive throughout, and
after, all that pain. I hadn't been able to confirm the accuracy of
the picture of the interrogation room that I had created in my
own mind the last time. Now I saw before me a corridor, which
was to be expected, but the interrogation room itself couldn't be
seen from where I was, though I could at least tell where it was.
I could tell that it was on the right, about five meters from the
beginning of the corridor. From the place where the room must
be a black shadow stretched over the ground, I didn't know whose.
It belonged to the person at whom the youth was looking as he
picked up what was left of his clothes. All he was wearing now
were black underpants and an undershirt whose color I couldn't
make out. He was holding a pile of clothes in his hands and water
was dripping from him. I quickly pushed the blindfold back over
my eyes and the privates brought the youth back to the truck. The
worst part began then; not when the privates dragged me by my
arms to the interrogation room but when they informed me that
we would be going straight back to the cell. What was I to tell
my companions when I arrived back there? That I'd been left in
the truck to listen to the screams of this young man? That they'd
spent the whole time torturing this unfortunate who'd committed
no crime and didn't want to waste five minutes on interrogating
me, even as a matter of routine? My being spared a beating the last
time hadn't been easy.

When we returned to the cell, I felt guilty and needed to offer
some explanation. Of course, I had no explanation, and despite my
fear as I listened to the youth's screams, I'd hoped that something
of the same sort would happen to me. That would be the only true
explanation for my being there, the only explanation that would
ensure that I wouldn't be asked to justify myself. If all I was to the
security forces was an extra burden, why didn't they get rid of me
and let me go? Why didn't they let me return to my family and just
bring me in when they had something worth punishing me for?
Maybe all they needed was a justification to do that. I didn't dare

offer them an excuse to beat me like the rest but I could offer them a justification for sending me back home.

I immediately asked to go in and see the officer. After a moment of silence, one of the goons said he'd inform him of my request. Waiting for him to come back, I wished I hadn't asked to go in, but the time passed. He took me inside the room. I was wearing the clothes I slept in, and my eyes, of course, were blindfolded. I was trembling so much from the cold that the air from the fan in the ceiling above me could almost have picked me up and thrown me down in some distant place. I told the officer that I wanted to go because my mother was sick and I wanted to see her. I heard a number of people laughing. He asked me who had told me this, and I said that a man had brought me books from my family and he had told me. The first part of my story was true. He asked me to describe the man, so I told him that I hadn't seen him because he'd talked to me through a small opening in the door. The officer told me to describe the opening, then burst into laughter, along with the others, while I trembled from the cold, the fear, and my embarrassment at the situation I'd got myself into. I repeated that it was a small opening in the door. He asked me to describe the man's mouth, then burst out laughing again. He asked me who'd guarantee to him that I'd come back to prison. I said, "You know my address. All I want is a few hours to see my mother. Then I'll come back." They were all splitting their sides with laughter and the officer told me, "Go away, kid. Go away and don't be so stupid."

The following day the poor young man was released, after all that beating and torture, which he had suffered because perhaps, really not knowing anything, he'd given answers that made the interrogator believe that he wasn't taking him seriously, or perhaps because he'd fallen into the hands of one of those interrogators who feel pangs of conscience – because they aren't carrying out their duty to the full – if they don't beat up those who come their way in order to get at least something out of them.

I was also taken, because of a mixup, for a third nighttime interrogation. The newest group to reach the security forces camp consisted of fifteen students from the Muslim Brotherhood. When they arrived, we were transferred from the solitary confinement cell that Majed and I were in to a large cell that could hold us all. At night, they came to summon the new arrivals to be interrogated. I was sitting chanting with them, so one of the privates made me stand up and pushed me into their midst.

The interrogation of the Muslim Brotherhood was nothing compared to that of the Jama'a Islamiya members, the reason being that the government regarded the Jama'a as an armed and present danger. The only similarity was that I was, again, blindfolded. The officer asked me who the leader of the Muslim Brotherhood at the university was and I said I didn't know. Someone close by hit me hard with a broad belt on my backside and back. The officer repeated his question and I repeated my answer. For the interrogator, this was just an introductory question and by denying I knew the answer I was simply pretending to be stupid. In vain, I tried to convince him that I wasn't a member of the Muslim Brotherhood, while he thought that I was denying my connection to them the way any arrested member of a given group would. I told him, "You can check, sir. I was arrested for membership in the Jama'a Islamiya, not the Brotherhood." The beating with the belt continued while the interrogator made a telephone call to check whether what I said was true. When he had confirmed that, he started asking me questions about the Jama'a Islamiya – stupid questions of course, given that the latter wasn't his area of expertise. They went on beating me with the belt, since it's difficult to give a convincing answer to a stupid question.

We returned to the cell laughing. Some couldn't sit down and others couldn't walk on the soles of their feet, so they took to hopping around like crows. It was my first night of good company with people I could tell stories to and joke with after spending a full ten days with Majed in a single cell. Along with the new arrivals came one individual from the Jama'a Islamiya, another Majed, who was two years younger than I and whom I'd got to know in the week at the university before I was arrested. He was tubby, with a childish face that never stopped smiling. I was sent with him to Luman Tura and I returned with him to Asyut and we were released the same day. He, however, was killed a few months later by the security forces, along with six others. The security forces had started to implement their new policy of immediate killing or imprisonment without set term, in the former case claiming each time that the dead men had opened fire first. They never, however, answered the simple question, "How could a group of seven persons open fire first, and thus possess the element of surprise, and yet not kill a single policeman?"

This was the first night I'd seen electric light since I'd come to the prison. The new cell contained numerous bunk beds which, however, had no bedding and had been reduced to their iron frames. It was my bad luck that I had to sleep beneath a long rusty bar. Half asleep, I got up in a panic when a cockroach walked along the bar and came so close to me that its antennae almost brushed my face. When Majed the Pious saw my terror, he laughed and said to me, "In our old cell there were cockroaches like that and plenty of them. The only difference was that we couldn't see them in the dark. Close your eyes and imagine you're in a cell without light."

It was a Wednesday night, which meant that the next morning would be a Thursday. Would that everything in the world could be like these universals, self-managing and routine! This was my second Thursday in captivity and, as on the first, my companions and I were fasting. We were let out of the cells at about ten in the morning and made to stand in two groups. Fifteen individuals from the Muslim Brotherhood were put into a large personnel carrier, while we, the seven members of the Jama'a Islamiya, were shackled together in a smaller truck. Each of us was attached by handcuffs to the persons on either side of him. The first and last persons in the chain were lucky, as each had one hand free. We chose to continue the fast, on a supererogatory basis, although we were traveling and prisoners. Eight hours later, when the time came to break the fast, we asked the officers to give us water but they refused. They were punishing us because of something else, another choice we had made, and we didn't break our fast until we reached the prison four hours later. If I had arrived merely with the fatigue of travel and of the handcuffs on my hands for ten straight hours, and the inability to move to the right or left in the truck, I wouldn't have felt that I'd done anything remarkable. We know that the Prophet (pbuh) has said, "To fast while traveling is not a pious act," but someone who wants to maximize his heavenly reward has different calculations.

This wasn't the only reason that I felt I'd done something worthwhile. The other reason was that other choice. The senior brother – who had been with us at the beginning when we were interrogated by the prosecutor and then spent a period incarcerated pending further interrogation – sought our advice as to whether we should call out our slogans when our truck passed through the middle of a town. It was his opinion that we should but I thought we shouldn't, because we were shackled and wouldn't be able to defend ourselves if they beat us up. Each one of us had his point of view. Majed the Pious said, "Let us ask God for guidance." It was a different sort of response, whose impact could be seen straightaway in the eyes of the senior brother, who looked with admiration at this youth who was willing to deliver his entire fate into the hands of God and refused to take a decision without recourse to the Lord; would that all humankind might do as he had, simultaneously, and with each decision! Should this happen, they would find themselves enveloped in a divine light that would never be interrupted and never lead astray. Majed closed his eyes, murmured a prayer, and then sat unmoving, to seek within his heart whatever God might inspire him with. All eyes were trained on him. "Let us call out!" he said, and as soon as Majed uttered these words with which God had inspired him, our throats opened: "On God's path we march, to raise the flag we strive! Not for party work we, for religion we give our lives!" and "Islamic! Islamic! Not socialist, not democratic!" – the same slogans that I used to hear when the personnel carriers would pass me in the street, strong slogans that shook my body and soul. This time I was one of them; I was a source of these cries. I was not the only one in our group who had maintained that we shouldn't call out; did this mean that I was one of a new species of criers whose cries would not inspire in others the confidence that their predecessors had inspired in me? In the end, I felt grateful that there were individuals among us such as Majed the Pious who could counter the defeatists among us, such as myself, and drag us kicking and screaming to the right choice.

We were taken first to Abu Za'bal prison, where the members of the Muslim Brotherhood were handed over to their jailers, and then we continued to Luman Tura prison. I expected another 'reception party' but it didn't happen. In fact, we were taken to a room where we handed over our clothes, and I personally handed in twenty pounds I had on me, while hiding twenty more beneath the inner sole of my trainers. I put on the prison clothes, which were made of thick linen like that used to make sacks for cotton, and colored beige. Then the guards led us to the wing with the solitary confinement cells (cells, that is, that had been built to hold one person but in which the increased number of inmates had forced the government to put five, or sometimes more). I traversed a long corridor with streaks of light that emanated from the cells that lined its right side like tombs, while along the left side ran a high wall that, it being night, I believed had nothing behind it but which turned out the following day to have been built to prevent the prisoners in the cells from seeing the prison yard. In the darkened corridor, the arrival of new prisoners was a source of celebration for the older inmates, whose voices came to us through the cell windows from heads looking out through the bars. "Where are you from, sheikh? What's your name, sheikh? Come and stay with us, sheikh!"

Choosing was difficult and depended in most cases on intuition – the way people spoke, their friendliness, whether one felt at home with them. The only thing that I was sure of was that I'd avoid staying in the same cell with Majed the Pious; our ten-day companionship had been enough. I felt that he was truly a good person and deserved only good, but I didn't want to be in the same place with him – a poor reason, but one not to be discounted, at least in comparison with the other factor that determined my choices: the dialect of Cairo made me feel at ease when I met someone else who spoke it; it was my dialect, which had made me stand out in at least one particular of life in Upper Egypt. It was especially important here as the light shining from behind their heads hid the features of the people in the cells, and it was this dialect that made the insistent invitation of one of the brothers more appealing to me than that of others, so that I chose to join him. I hadn't expected him to be on his own, but I was surprised to find, given that the surface area of the cell wasn't more than two meters by two, one third of which at least was taken up by the toilet, that there were three others with him. As I entered, I noticed the annoyance of two of the inmates.

After the introductions, I told them that I had been fasting and hadn't had anything to eat or drink till now, the time then being close to midnight, so they brought me all the leftover food they'd been able to put aside – peas and feta cheese. The cheese carton had been pressed flat. A piece had been cut off one side and the cheese came out like crème Chantilly from a funnel. I don't know why this made it taste even better. All the food in that prison tasted better, especially given that I'd spent the first ten days in the security forces camp practically without food. The prison meal consisted of not much more than a cupful of stewed beans and four loaves, which we received in the morning five days a week; on the two remaining days, it was a cupful of rice and one of lentils. This mixture of white and yellow, made without spices, was like a feast-day meal. I'd often heard about the weevil-filled prison beans, but when I saw the beans I told the brothers I'd eat them as they were, as they looked normal and I was too lazy to pick through my food every day to get rid of the weevils. The brothers let me do as I pleased the first day, but the next they insisted that I try picking through them just once, after which I could do as I liked. I was amazed at the quantity of weevils that I removed, of which I must have eaten a similar quantity the previous day. In my first letter, I wrote to my mother, "Before, I used to think that the weevils bored into the beans and lived inside them. Here, I've learned that they swallow the beans." Even those beans, however, could be transformed into tasty and interesting food. Brothers from another Islamist group based in Bani Soueif lived in the cell above ours, on the upper floor, which my companions regarded as a five-star hotel. Its cells had primitive electric hotplates, smuggled in by the brothers; these would be confiscated in the inspections that the prison administration conducted and then the brothers would pay bribes to the guards to get them new hotplates, and so it went. From time to time, these brothers on the upper floor would let down to us a rope and one of us would stand on the shoulders of another in order to grab it through the window, which was small and had been cemented up by the administration except for a small area at the top, a space just large enough to allow the passage of a family-size plastic Pepsi bottle. We would fill the latter with beans, then tie it to a rope dangling down from the cell above, and give it a jerk so that the people there would start raising it. Upstairs, they'd put some tomatoes into oil and leave them for a while over the heat. Then they'd add the beans and some spices and return it to us by the same means, accompanied this time by a smell to whet the appetite, and a rich taste.

On some occasions, we'd receive gift packages of food containing pasta and chicken or meat. The first time this happened, the package was intended for one of the two brothers from Cairo who were in the cell – a youth in his twenties who had grown up without a mother and been raised by his father's second wife, of whom he always spoke well and whom he always referred to as 'my mother.' This boy, who was from Imbaba (designated 'the Islamic Republic of Imbaba' by the Egyptian media because of the influence of the Jama'a followers there), had been arrested because he had given his I.D. card to a brother who had been in hiding from the security forces for ten years. The fugitive had intended to use it to forge a passport on which he could leave Egypt, probably to go to Saudi Arabia and from there to Afghanistan, this being the route we knew the brothers who had fought with the mujahidin to have taken, but the police arrested the fugitive one day before the plan was to be put into action, when he went to say goodbye to his mother-in-law, whose house was under surveillance. The brother who owned the I.D. was then brought to State Security. Another brother in the cell told me that this brother from Imbaba had arrived in an appalling condition from the State Security headquarters in Lazoghli where he'd been locked up with his hands and feet in shackles for two weeks and where, after torturing him, they'd refused to allow him to use the toilet, so that he'd defecated and urinated on himself.

The man's 'mother' went to all the trouble of visiting him in
Luman Tura from time to time, usually returning without having
been able to see him, in which case she would send the food to
the cell. This first time when I was present, he wept when the food
was brought to him, explaining to me that he was conscious of his
family's poverty and that they couldn't afford such expenses, but
were having to bear the cost of the choices he had made. Despite
all the care that had been taken, the brothers discovered that the
pasta had gone off but we ate it all the same. My appetite for food
was, it seems, too big to be catered for by what the prison could
provide, and this became one of the many secrets, large and small,
that were carried back and forth between one cell and another,
rarely with malicious intent and generally as a product of the
endless empty days, which could be spent only stretched out on
the floor. In this position, one's feet almost touched the door, while
one's head almost touched the opposite wall. The inmate would
rest his head on one of his arms and, with the other, take hold of
a pen or a spoon or whatever else was available and dig into the
wall that separated him from the next cell. After a month or two of
effort from either side, a hole the size of half a face would be made,
exactly in front of the place where one's head was when sleeping,
so that the brother had no need to get up or sit upright in order to
communicate with 'the outside world.' When I got to the prison,
the hole in our cell was already there. Through it Brother Usama
from Alexandria was able to tell the inmate in the next cell that I'd
polished off all the food in the cell, and it was through it too that
another brother told me jokingly what Usama had told him, after
the latter had left our cell. I felt extremely embarrassed, despite
the fact that the whole thing was probably no more than a joke.
For Upper Egyptians, however, to eat with appetite in "the house
of strangers" is not a sign of hunger, but rather a faux pas, and this
was something I considered important.

Ahmad, the other Alexandrian in the cell, was completely illit-
erate and worked as a car mechanic. Usama, on the other hand,
had an intermediate qualification. Ahmad was the exact opposite
of someone like me who had been brought up under the wing of
parents both of whom were university graduates, both of whom

had studied for and obtained postgraduate degrees and whose first priority in life had been to ensure that their children obtained the best education possible. During the first days in the cell, and especially after just me and the two Alexandrians were left, I felt that Usama was closer to me. He, for example, called his mother and father 'Mama' and 'Baba,' as I did. He was picky too, and wanted everything to be as clean as if he were living at home. We quickly became rivals, however, competing at doing as little as we could. Ahmad (how embarrassing!) volunteered to clean the toilet for us, and, when I washed my underclothes for the first time in my life and scratched the back of my hand, he swore that I should never wash them again and he would wash them for me. He would see me crying as I wrote letters to my parents and pretend to be asleep so that I wouldn't feel embarrassed. When my school books reached me, he kept silent for the longest period possible so that I'd be able to study my lessons, and I know how cruel not being able to talk was when conversation was the sole means of consuming the seconds, minutes, hours, and days, and was the sole means of expressing one's dudgeon and boredom and pain and anger. I told Ahmad that I'd heard Usama telling the residents of the neighboring cells through the hole in the wall the names of brothers who had, under torture, implicated others, and Ahmad told me that he had with his own ears heard Usama himself implicating him, Ahmad, when the officer had taken him into the interrogation room. This made me feel that I had repaid Usama's insult. When I first met my cell mates, however, it never occurred to me that anything so trivial could preoccupy us; neither the four faces that I beheld nor the opening in the wall led me to think that. I had expected great, or more dramatic, things, things as clear as night and day, or the days of the week. We, together, were on one side, and the enemy beyond these walls was on the other. And when, on my first night, I woke with a shock to the screams of our fourth cellmate, one of them whispered to me, "Don't worry. Ever since he came from Lazoghli he's been like that." I was afraid but I felt comforted. This was a confrontation that didn't exhaust one with calculations.

The brother who screamed in his sleep was a man of great

generosity, open-handed and chivalrous, but he couldn't recite the
Qur'an well or speak on any of the Islamic sciences when we held a
study session. I led them in prayer, though, given the limited area
of the cell, I could stand only a few centimeters in front of them.
I was, therefore, aware of his fidgetiness when I made them linger
too long over the noon prayer. He asked me why I drew it out
so, and I told him that Sheikh Umar Abd el-Rahman read to the
brothers in prison a *rub'* of the Qur'an at each prostration, and he
said no more. There was, though, another reason, which I didn't
mention: the brothers in the next-door cell (the one on the toilet
side this time) had informed me that Majed spent hours praying
and was an exemplary leader who organized for them Qur'an reci-
tation sessions and study sessions. I didn't want to be any less than
him; I wanted to make a new beginning, through which I would
teach myself true devotion:

> If you are not like them, imitate them;
> In the imitation of the righteous salvation lies.

In any case, nature is stronger than nurture, and I was not a naturally devout person. This was not something I'd ever hid from the
brothers, and they had accepted it, on the basis that the history
of Islam was not a history of devout worshipers. There were
the mujahidin, who brought religion its domination, and there
were the memorizers of the Qur'an and the jurisprudents, who
preserved its creed. I wanted to be like Sayyid Qutb one day. I
too started fidgeting and shortening the prayer. This particular
brother, though, joined the man from Cairo and left our cell.

After six days in Luman Tura, the headache got the better of
me. I knew that it was a symptom of depression, but this knowledge was of no help in getting rid of it. A brother who was a doctor
used to come by, so I, like the others, stepped onto a blanket that
we had folded into a triangle, the ends of whose long side we then
tied to the bars at either end of the opening in the cell door thus
making a 'V' shape whose point was twenty centimeters from the
floor. This was necessary in order for me to bring my eyes and
mouth to the level of the opening and thus be able to make my

pains public. I told the doctor and he replied, "Psychic," which is what he said to all those whom I heard tell him their symptoms. I wanted to get out of the cell if only for quarter of an hour and go to the prison clinic, perhaps just to give my feet a walk or perhaps to talk to a doctor who would show a little concern. The fact that a headache has psychosomatic origins by no means removes the need for it to be treated. I got angrily off the blanket, sat resting my back on the wall opposite the door, and started crying from the headache. Ahmad tried to persuade the doctor to send me to the clinic but without success.

I don't know where Sayyid Qutb found the moral strength to be able to complete all those volumes in prison. Earlier, I had sent my family three letters, and didn't know which had arrived and which had not. That was not my basic concern. Writing in and of itself was the best occupation in prison, using up the time, preserving, so far as was possible, my mental and psychological balance, and giving me some hope of escape from this world of the bad and the worse. It helped me to create tunes to accompany the monotonous noise in which I swam and give value to the nothingness that I inhabited and that inhabited me. I didn't write ordinary letters but poetic odes that spread over pages that, to this day, I don't know how I managed to find the news to fill. I would keep writing for hours on end. I slept and woke early so that I could finish a letter. Once, when the brother who collected our letters came by, I asked Ahmad, who was standing on the blanket, to give him my letter, but he refused to take it, saying, "Give it to the postman."

This sarcastic formula was an example of Egyptian wit, no doubt, but not of the spontaneous kind. Nor was it likely that an individual, charged by the Jama'a with seeing to "the business of the Muslims," would take a decision of this sort on his own authority. I had suspicions that could not be proven, and *certain suspicions are sins* (Qur'an 49:12). Maybe I had gone too far in writing such long letters and in so doing had encroached on others' share of letter sending. If I wanted to kill time, there were other things I could do, things that would strengthen ties with the others and not imprison me within myself. I wanted to be imprisoned with Sheikh Mahmud, my ideal Jama'a member. I had believed, before going there, that prison was cut off from the world but open to the prisoners, but even this hope turned out not to be true. There was no leaving the ground-floor individual cells, no hour's exercise time, not even five minutes to walk in the corridor. When I looked through the bars on the door, I would lean right and left, trying to change the angle of vision so that I could see an additional course of stones, or some writing made by a brother on a cement wall that I had not noticed before. The leaders, such as Sheikh Mahmud, were doubly isolated, being kept in a distant part of the prison so that they could not mix with the 'common brothers,' either in the individual cells or even on the upper floor, whose inmates were allowed to go down for an hour's exercise and sometimes to play soccer. I couldn't see them because of the wall that hid the courtyard from us but I could hear the sound of the ball being kicked from foot to foot, of feet running, and of their shouts as they called back and forth – groans at lost chances, cheers for goals. There was no hope of seeing Sheikh Mahmud but at least I could communicate with those of that group that I knew. From time to time one of the brothers from the upper floor would climb down onto the top of the wall that divided us from the courtyard to ask about our needs and that was an excellent opportunity for some general conversation and for asking about particular people. I asked to see Sheikh Ashraf, whom I knew well from Asyut. The brother went back and then returned to inform me that Ashraf was "a little dizzy" and couldn't come down. The reply didn't reassure me. The next time Ashraf came down onto the wall, I quickly stepped up onto the blanket and looked out, a broad smile on my face. He stayed a while talking to Majed without turning his glance the slight degree needed to see and greet me. The moment he finished, I greeted him and he returned my greeting. Then he left, saying he had to go right back upstairs. *Certain suspicions are sins* but my suspicions weren't to be numbered among those. I received a letter from Sheikh Mahmud that said, "If your care is all for this world and you think you can study in prison and thus succeed and get good marks, you are mistaken."

✳

Lazoghli was the place I had most wanted to avoid since arrival at Luman

Tura. What frightened me most about it was the thought of being on my own there, of being detached from the phalanx in which our bodies and minds were arrayed in solid rows, to face the unknown on my own. New arrivals came and went. I would wake up and find new faces in the cell, and sometimes I'd look for a face and not find it. They would inform me that he had "gone to Lazoghli" and I'd pray that God would make things easy for him, begging Him to spare me from hearing my name called. Lazoghli remained, however, a constant presence. Fear of it allowed me to sympathize with the brothers' behavior. In such circumstances, we could not indulge in the luxury of individual differences. We could not allow the enemy to seduce us into displays of weakness. We might confront ourselves and enter into self-questioning and doubt, for sure, but we couldn't make this public. We might confront one another and differ, like any human beings, but we couldn't turn conflicts among individuals into enmities that might eat away at the body of the Jama'a. We were not a political party or a corporation; our aspirations were universal and concerned the future of humankind. We were the Word of God that must remain, whatever the individual cost. I had not been dealt with in a hostile manner for personal reasons or even for my behavior, but for the cost of that behavior. Expelling me from the phalanx had become less of a burden for them than including me in it. Did I long for my family, from whom I was separated for the first time in my life? Everyone else had families too. The universe would collapse if they all shed tears the way I did. Did I complain of a headache brought on by claustrophobia and depression? I was not the only one. No one could be the only one. Here the individual and the group entered the decisive confrontation together. Great issues against petty matters. This face-off had to be resolved decisively if we wanted an opportunity to bring to a head the only true confrontation, which was that between us and the real enemy. And you would know who the true enemy was if, God forbid, you should be taken to Lazoghli. Then you would see your wants in proper perspective.

The only thing I wanted was for someone to talk to me, to make me feel, by any means, that my presence in this place was known, that the address of the prison was known, and the location of my cell. There were a few things in my life that merited nostalgia: my sister's son, Ziyad, was a year and a half old when I was arrested; he was the first child born in our home when I was of an age to be aware of such things. Recently he had learned to walk, and his head was completely bald, like a taro tuber. I kept his picture with me always. This yearning for family was something even I had never expected. I would lose an academic year, though I had been able to get through those preceding it only at the cost of great effort inside and outside the university. I would also lose a love that I had previously still held out some hope for. There were other things too, which were at variance with my ever-present shyness but which I could not divulge, for I had been brought up in a household where none of us ever saw another less than fully clothed. Here, however, I would get nervous whenever I saw that Ahmad – who to that point had spent six months in the prison – would spend a not inconsiderable amount of time indulging in the "secret habit." I would catch sight of the movement of his hand under a cover that he used to hide himself with and, in the silence of the day or the quiet of the night, hear his sighing in the toilet, which was a part of the cell. Even the toilet was a source of worry, and I would never use it until my stomach was on the brink of bursting. My mind was on the brink of bursting too. If I went to Lazoghli, I would understand the difference between the easy and the petty, between cost and value.

I heard my name called for the first time since I had entered this box – my name in full. Like a house cat, I went on the alert while staying rooted to the spot. When the name was repeated a number of times, I jumped onto the blanket and called out to the guard, who was trying his luck at finding me elsewhere along the corridor. He came to me eagerly and told me, as he inserted the key in the lock, "They want you at Lazoghli." Ahmad hugged me and made light of it. Everything would be fine and I shouldn't worry. But I did worry, and I walked the distance from the cell to the corridor as though I were being led away to my execution. My legs wrapped themselves around one another and the sweat poured from my forehead. I wondered whether the brothers had any hand in this – pushing me into what I feared so that I could overcome it. I wondered in what state I would return, if I ever did return. With faeces and urine all over my clothes? As a victim of a sexual assault that would destroy my self-respect? I hadn't been tortured in Asyut because they were saving up the real interrogation for Lazoghli. The basic thing that I'd learned from the Asyut interrogations was that I knew nothing. And I knew one other thing, which was that those who knew nothing were tortured more if the interrogator believed, or someone informed him, that they knew something.

When I reached the end of the corridor, I looked about me. I was looking for human beings of a different kind. For sure, the persons who took people to Lazoghli would look unlike any others. All I could see was the guard who had brought me from the cell. He laughed. "You have a lawyer's visit," he said. I didn't know whether to hug him or spit on him. I was grateful but at the same time felt an overwhelming resentment toward this man who had taken it upon himself to scare me without anyone having asked him to do so, and without there being anything of benefit in it for him.

The lawyer gave me a pair of pants, which was all that the prison administration had allowed me, of a pajama set sent to me by my parents, along with underwear and some academic books, and informed me that he had made a deposit of fifty pounds in my name. I could now buy some extra food. Before doing so, however, I was going to take a shower and change my clothes for the first time in seventeen days.

Ahmad's color had changed in the quarter of an hour I'd been away. When the guard opened the cell door for me, he was sitting in the corner next to the opening in the wall. He had already told the inmates of the next door cell that I had been summoned to Lazoghli, and now he announced the good news that it was a false alarm. The false alarm indeed merited celebration: from now on I would no longer worry over being summoned to go to Lazoghli – I had already been summoned. A false alarm? So be it, but it had happened. Also, the lawyer's visit meant that my presence in this place was now an established fact. At the least, my parents would know if anything bad happened to me. I wouldn't need to write letters to them anymore, and I wouldn't need to talk to Ashraf. If I were outside, I wouldn't even ask to see him. In Asyut, he'd tried to imitate Sheikh Mahmud's style of preaching but he lacked the authentic human touch that the sheikh possessed. I would talk only to Sheikh Mahmud, if I met him, because I knew that his harshness wasn't an exercise of power but of love – a lesson in love a person cannot learn when he is out of breath from running after power, or he will choke.

As for the cough that I had caught in the security forces camp in Asyut and which had got worse here, it was no psychosomatic symptom. When it became unbearable to me and to the others, they took me to the prison clinic. On the way back, one of the inmates of the upper floor signaled to me to make my way straight to the gate that opened onto his floor, as though I were one of its inmates. Even after I'd been living on the ground floor for two weeks, the guards didn't notice that one of their charges had hood-winked them and joined 'the people upstairs.' This move calmed somewhat my fears that the cough, which had lasted two weeks, would develop into another, with blood, and that analysis would indicate that I had tuberculosis, for all the conditions on the lower floor seemed to have been designed especially to preserve the germs of that disease from extinction. Naturally, the fact that I had studied medicine made me fall victim to the suspicions that afflict all those who study it. I remembered that tuberculosis was a so-called socioeconomic disease that spreads in conditions of poor ventilation and deficient nutrition. The upper floor was something entirely different, though. At least there one was allowed an hour's exercise time, which we took on alternate days, which meant that we got a breath of fresh air. Even more important, it had a radio, on which I heard for the first time a voice from the outside world. I could also read newspapers. They were two weeks old but they were still newspapers.

The cells were spacious, and a quantity of cardboard sheets was enough to serve as mattresses that kept our bodies from the damp of the floor. There was also a wire that brought in electricity, and we would put its ends into a large plastic vessel full of water, so that we could bathe in hot water.

*

It was not my turn to go out for exercise that day, and I stayed in the cell on my own. I went to put the electric wire in the heating bucket but by mistake it fell onto the plastic instead of into the water and the container burst into flame. I didn't know what to do. I was afraid to beat out the fire with a blanket and spill the water, which was in contact with the wire, onto the floor and perhaps electrocute myself, and I couldn't get close enough to the high flames to take hold of the wire. I ran to the door of the cell and yelled through the opening, "Fire! Fire! Help!" but no one heard me. I went back gingerly to the furthest place from the fire from which I could get a hold of the wire, twisted a piece of cardboard into a stick, removed the wire with it, and then carefully brought it close to me so that I could grab it with my hand. If it were to slip from the stick and touch the ground ... ! All the lessons of physics came back to me. Then I went up to the bucket and gave it a kick, and the water poured onto the flame and extinguished it. I could have done all this at the start, but the feeling of impotence turns even the simplest of accidents in prison into fearful monsters in just the same way that the blind man trembles at a strange sound and the cripple finds himself incapable of reaching something that is only a hand's span out of reach.

With us in the cell was a brother who was a dentist and never stopped talking, moving from topic to topic in a way that made it impossible for anyone to concentrate. Short and a little plump, he had a beard that encircled his face as neatly as though he had had the ends trimmed by a barber. On my first day with them, he insisted on teaching me how to give an injection, something which, he said, could on occasion save a life, especially in prison, and which I, as a third-year medical student, ought to know how to do. He took hold of the hand of a brother who was complaining of a pain in his belly, stretched out his arm in front of me, and taught me how to choose the right vein and how to give the jab at an angle that wouldn't cause the patient any pain. He told me how to draw out a little blood so as to be sure that the needle was in the center of the vein and then deliver the injection slowly. Then he said to the brother, in the tones of a teacher wrapping up his lesson, "If you feel a spasm or there is pain or numbness, let us know immediately." I put the needle as instructed into the anxious brother's arm and the second I exerted pressure, he yelled that his hand was tingling. I immediately pulled my hand away and left the needle swaying this way and that. The dentist then intervened and completed the injection, reproaching the brother for his reaction and me for leaving the syringe in his arm like that.

I loved the humorous spirit of this company. I didn't have a loofah and during one shower dropped three pieces of soap into the toilet bowl because they were impossible to hold onto. The brothers then punished me by making me bathe without soap from then on. We had a brother from a village in the north of Egypt with us, from Sharqiya to be precise, and he had a distinctive accent. The Cairene 'q' and 'g' and the Upper Egyptian 'j' all coexisted peacefully in his dialect. None of us, whether from the north or the south, could understand this accent that exploded all the unwritten rules of our colloquial language. This same village brother, who always sat crossed-legged, his hands together in his lap as though listening to a sermon, absolutely refused to eat halva, a food whose taste is so closely associated with prisons in Egypt that the phrase 'bread and halva' has come to mean 'prison'; he used to say that eating it led to wet dreams and these would require that he perform a complete ritual ablution before the dawn prayer. The latter was usually done with cold water as none of the half-asleep worshipers had the patience to wait for the water to heat before the prayer was underway. As halva constituted half the food of the prison and half the food that came in the form of care packages, this was a real problem, and there was a never-ending debate between the man and the dentist over how to solve it that had, with time, shifted from joking to feuding. The dentist told me that he knew I would appreciate his position as he was like Sheikh Mahmud (of my relationship to whom I had often spoken to him) and couldn't stand stupidity. Outside of the prison, I might have objected to this characterization but inside anything went. Benign gossip was particularly pleasant – eight individuals in a cell who saw one another night and day, and who looked one another up and down, and down and up.

"That's how people in Maadi think," was one of the favorite formulas with which another brother liked to bring his words to a close, whenever he offered an opinion in a discussion. He had other similar formulas too, such as, "Did you think that just because I'm from Maadi I wouldn't be observant?" Maadi is one of Cairo's affluent districts and its residents are held up as representatives of a luxurious lifestyle reminiscent of that of the west. What I loved about that brother was how lively he was, as though he had just this second come from dancing in a wedding procession. If I addressed him, he would jump up and come and stand close to me, pushing out his chest and presenting a picture of rapt attention, as though he and I were preparing a secret plan and agreeing on the password. He used one of his Maadi-ite catchphrases in debate with another brother from Cairo, who then asked him, "Where exactly are you from in Maadi?" and the questions continued with an increasing geographic precision that meant nothing to me until the enquirer arrived at the fact that the first brother lived in the area known as Maadi Gardens, which is a low-class neighborhood close to the original Maadi; in fact, he lived in the most low-class part of that neighborhood. I don't believe that the brother from Maadi was trying to give an impression of a fictitious class affiliation. In our conversations he said frankly that his mother was a seamstress and, as the Egyptians have it, had to "run after her bread." The whole thing, as I see it, came down to the fact that living in Maadi was something he loved and that gave him something to be happy about, as a sort of compensation for the good things in life that he'd missed out on since coming to the prison.

The Jama'a Islamiya, as a part of Egyptian society with all its contradictions, is by no means, however, without aspects of class distinction. The difference is that these operate more flexibly there. Offspring of the 'rich' classes who were committed to the Jama'a were used as an example of the insignificance of the concept of class and of the triviality of this world, as manifested in wealth and standing, in the eyes of the Jama'a. The example of Saudi millionaire Usama bin Ladin was so used, as was that of certain homegrown notables. The offspring of the poorer classes who had reached positions of responsibility within the Jama'a were held up as examples of the Jama'a's impartiality and thus also of the model society which it strove to create. Between these two ideals there were, as in any society, class-based pretensions from above and below: some from a poor background were ashamed of their background and some from the middle classes would also seek to deny theirs. With all due respect to the many studies that point to the economic element as a factor in the phenomenon of the Jama'a Islamiya, offering as evidence statistics on the number of committed members of the Islamist movement vis-à-vis their educational and social backgrounds, I believe that these studies fail to take into account the divide between the Jama'a's leadership hierarchy and the vast mass of its adherents. The primary motor of the Jama'a's work consists almost entirely of university graduates. I try so far as is possible to avoid theorizing, but what I felt when a committed member of the Jama'a and remain convinced of to this day is that political Islam is a reflection of the crisis of the middle class in societies in which this class, and those below it, have lost their faith in social mobility as a key to future opportunities.

However much I enjoyed my life in this cell, my studies still kept me awake at night. How was I supposed to study in a cell where there was no source of entertainment besides conversation, a situation for which one could not hold its inmates responsible? The dentist's attempts to help me by explaining some of the lessons were no use, for I'm one of those people who cannot concentrate if someone nearby is whispering. Never in my life, or only rarely, did I study to the sound of music or the radio or even with a friend. Reviewing what I had learned meant to me a piece of paper and a pen with which I wrote down every point that I understood in the way that I understood it and which I used to expose every point that I found difficult to understand. It was the first week of November and the academic year was just beginning. It seemed very likely that the university students in prison would continue the academic year once they were released; the policy of incarcerating 'ordinary' members of the Jama'a for years had not yet begun. This led to the brothers' decision to redistribute some of us among the cells, particularly with a view to gathering the students in one cell, thus providing them with an appropriate atmosphere for study. All of them would be under the supervision of one brother, who was not a student.

There were three Secondary school brothers from Alexandria with me in the cell. To me, they seemed like children. I don't say that here to demean them but as a way of expressing my affection for them, which also included a dose of pity. I had passed the Secondary General exam only three years before, in the year following my transfer from my old school and the year following my choice as amir of the Secondary chool brothers. I had felt at that time a great sense of responsibility and had borne on my shoulders and in my heart a sense of concern and feelings of guilt and blame that bore no relationship to what I saw in the faces before me now. Did they feel as I had? And had I looked as they did? I, like them, had had no beard three years before and certainly they, like me, must have had their sights set on achieving a good result in that year that is so crucial within the Egyptian school system. When I was in Secondary General school, I, however bad everything may have been, was at liberty. I was capable, to some degree, of sorting out my priorities, of distancing myself temporarily from the brothers, no matter who might disapprove. I had a house and a room of my own to study in and I had parents to pay for whatever private tutoring I might need. I had a school to go to and a bed to relax on after all that effort. These boys, though, who were still fighting their schoolboy fights and throwing paper darts at one another, had nothing of that. That may explain why they liked to play much more than to study. Another brother, who was studying engineering, and I became very fed up with our role as "the old folk at the wedding": "Come on now, quieten down a bit. Come on now, do sit down and study."

The cell leader was a quiet brother, thin and short. He spoke in a low voice and would nod his head as one talked to him, as though he understood what one was trying to say. He would listen to you to the end, then give his opinion tersely and get up and turn his back on you and go somewhere else in the cell, as though he had an appointment. He set study hours for us, specifying when to start and when to stop, and where each of us was to sit. He decided that we should all eat using the only spoon in the cell, passing it from mouth to mouth, which was something I had never done before. This same leader had a glandular dysfunction that made his mouth fill with saliva all the time and that is what made me agree to eat with the same spoon – the sense of guilt: if I refused, he would think I had done so because of his problem and that would upset him in a way that I didn't want to.

Nevertheless, I asked the brothers to send me back to my previous cell, and the same day the brother in charge of the upper-floor cells, Brother Sayyid from Bani Soueif, informed me that they had prepared another arrangement, namely my transfer to his cell, in order to assist me in being steadfast in the truth. We were standing in the corridor by which we went out for exercise and leaning on the wall from which one could look out over the main courtyard behind the prison gate. He revealed to me that the brothers had been opening my letters to my family and had deduced from them that I intended to leave the Jama'a, since I had asked my parents in one letter to make every effort to have my papers transferred to Cairo and said I'd give them all the guarantees they wanted and would submit to their conditions. The period I'd spent on the upper floor had helped me to calm down and pull myself together. One day before this conversation, I had seen Sheikh Mahmud through the window in the door of the students' cell greeting other prisoners, from whom he was separated only by the door to that wing of the prison. He was on his way back from the clinic and the brothers had gathered in large numbers to affectionately shake and kiss his hand. I yelled out with all my might, "Sheikh Mahmu-uuuud!" but of course he didn't hear me and didn't raise his eyes to the upper floor. I wasn't lying at all when I told Brother Sayyid that they were mistaken and that I'd never intended to leave the Jama'a. I told him too that the idea of my transfer from the University of Asyut to Cairo University had been a matter of discussion in my family since the year before and that Sheikh Mahmud, who had transferred his own papers to Zaqaziq, knew of the matter, for I wasn't the only brother to do this, given that life at the University of Asyut had become meaningless, what with the constant chases and the impossibility of attending lectures.

I gathered up my things and moved to the new cell. Brother Sayyid, whose face I knew from Asyut but with whom I hadn't been acquainted personally there, was pleasant, polite, and frank. This in turn encouraged me to talk to him openly of the questions that were going through my mind about the Islamist action and the absence of leadership on the outside, from my perspective, of course. He listened to me without interrupting, then told me we'd talk about the matter another time. He and another brother in the cell started a conversation about two groups in their hometown, Bani Soueif, one of which had murdered the amir of the other. Brother Sayyid said he had borrowed a book from a member of the group that had carried out the killing in the knowledge that it contained the religious arguments against what that group had done. By so doing, he had intended to create a context that would make it possible for him to talk with this individual and reproach him for their act. He was taken aback, however, to find written in the margin next to that argument a comment from which he inferred that the group that had carried out the killing had used that very same argument to justify the murder.

That night I woke to perform the dawn prayer, then went back to sleep. In a dream I saw myself crying. When I woke again in the morning to the voice of the prison guard calling my name, my pillow was wet. Brother Sayyid, who slept next to me, smiled and said, "The time of your release has come," and I answered spontaneously, still half asleep:

"By many a setback the young man, helpless,
Is beset that God alone can solve.
I was sore pressed, the chain forever tighter binding,
And then released, though I had thought my case could
never be resolved."

I looked through the window in the door of the cell and the guard said, "You?" "Yes," I said, and he responded, "Congratulations. You're to be released. Get yourself ready."

I took my things and went to the first room I had entered when I came to the prison. I got my money from the personal property section plus what was left of the money the lawyer had deposited for me; it was four pounds short, according to my calculations of the amounts that should have been deducted for the food I had bought. I changed my clothes. It's a wonderful thing that people do in their daily lives, to put on clothes that they themselves have chosen. Before I left to get into the transporter, one of the guards came up to me and asked, "Where are our tips?" "You put me in prison and you want tips too?" I responded.

From the vehicle, I could see life proceeding as normal, which I had thought it had stopped doing. I passed a school where the pupils were singing the national anthem and I cried. Not out of patriotism; it was just that I remembered myself as I was in Elementary school – the last time when you could sing the national anthem at the morning line-up without the others around you making fun of you. I felt sorry for the children who were walking beside the vehicle in their school uniforms. What would be their fate? Then I saw men and women talking and laughing and I felt grim enough to kill them without caring.

As darkness fell, I found myself returned to the police station from which my journey to prison had begun, and once again they took me from there to the Central Security forces camp. I thought they might be about to re-arrest me. This was the usual setup for re-arrests: you'd leave the official police station, then be held in some place where no records were kept, giving the impression that you'd been released; then you'd be re-arrested under a new decree that would initiate a fresh round of detention.

On 17 November 1991, an officer came and took me from my cell at the security camp and ordered me to face the wall, raise my hands, and spread my legs. Then he struck me with his stick and his hand. I don't know why. He didn't ask me any questions, he just hit me. Then he took me, blindfolded, in a police vehicle, from which I was taken down and led by a police private to a waiting area. The private pulled off the blindfold and I saw that I was in the State Security Police building. In the same place was a young man I didn't know with shaven beard and wearing pants and a shirt. It seemed he'd come to ask about a relative of his who was in prison. Before he left, I gave him a piece of paper with my family's telephone number and asked him to call them and tell them I was there. More than three hours later, a goon came, blindfolded me, and walked with me. He would tell me that here there was a staircase in front of me and that I was to raise my feet, then that I should turn to the right or left, then to put my head down as there was a low door in front of me. In the end, the blindfold was removed and I found myself in a room furnished with moderate luxury. A police inspector made me sit in a chair and ordered me tea. He was talking to someone whom I deduced must be an official on the teaching staff of the University of Asyut about the student security reports and what the policy on them should be. It was past one in the morning.

When he had finished talking to his last guest, he spoke to me about medical school, saying that people were falling over one another to get into it and speaking of the future that awaited me when I graduated as a doctor, and that he was obliged, to his sorrow, to inform me of the decision to bar me from the school for the period of a year. Then he gave me a piece of paper with his telephone number on it and asked me to call him if anyone tried to contact me or if I came into possession of information that might be detrimental to the country's security. I said that I wouldn't try to contact any member of the Jama'a but I wouldn't work as an informer, that I would concern myself with my studies only. The inspector told me that I had wronged my homeland and that I had to pay for my mistake by working for its good, like any citizen who loved Egypt.

I left the at office about two in the morning. I tore up the piece of paper and walked away fast, still feeling that this might be a trick so that they could re-arrest me, or at least that someone might arrest me simply for being a bearded individual walking in the street at that late hour. I didn't know whether to walk more slowly or to run. I trusted to my soccer instincts and ran. I cannot describe my feelings during those moments. I may get somewhere close to the truth if I say that I – the Islamic fundamentalist – felt at that instant that life was more beautiful than Paradise, and that the human soul dangles from the beak of the bird of freedom.

I reached home and my mother opened the door to me and embraced me, saying, "Dearie!" It occurred to me that this was a strange expression for my mother to use. She ought to have said, "My son!" In her choice of word, I felt an overwhelming tenderness.

5

Life

My room was as I had left it the day I was arrested. My mother had refused to move anything from its place. The folding table on wheels whose leaves I'd opened out the day I was arrested was still in front of the balcony. On the table, where my right-hand had rested was still a tea glass, narrow toward the bottom and widening like a flower toward the top, of a French make that broke only if it fell on its base. It was still half-filled with black tea, which had gone slightly green on the surface. The pillow was still in the same place on the bed, and the bed cover lay, untouched, in the position into which it had been kicked by my foot. My brother had an extra reason to long for my return: my mother had imposed a ban on my favorite foods throughout my absence. I for my part was longing for many things. The first thing I did was to save my parents the trouble of informing me that I had been suspended from college. Nothing could spoil my joy at being free and take away from me the warmth that came with laying my head on my own pillow and pulling up my own covers, or with rising from sleep and sitting on the 'Frankish'-style toilet and then washing with hot water and handling the clean, neatly arranged clothes in my own closet, or of re-arranging from time to time the desk and bed in my room, as I was given to doing. During my first hours, there was only one thing I took care to make sure I did, which was to see my paternal uncle who lived in the apartment next to ours and who is one of the people for whose presence in my life I will always feel grateful. His work as a judge had given him the capacity to listen. He always disagreed with me but he always respected my point of view. I had sent greetings in a letter while in prison to his son, Hazem, because he was "the only person of those around you who deserve them"; I was reproaching my uncle because he hadn't done what he could to spare me the experience of prison. I was wrong, of course. He had striven with all the means available to him to ensure that I was released. The fact is that he wasn't obligated to do anything; indeed, he of all people should have been spared having to intervene in a matter such as that. I discovered from my family that his wife had read my letter with my mother and that my uncle hadn't become angry with me for my reproaches; he had understood that my psychological state excused them, which was something I would come to appreciate greatly, especially during this period.

I longed to see the brothers and spend time with them, and the warmth of their welcome allayed any suspicions I might have had. I longed for the smell of the carpets in the mosque, a smell of dampness caused by the impress of feet after ablutions suffused with the smell of musk from hands pressed upon them during the worshipers' prostrations. I longed for the clear silence that brings a tinge of beige to the world, the strained calm of the seasonal sandy winds that herald the coming of springtime in my home-town. And I longed for the university, whose inaccessibility to me now made it more desirable to me than ever before. Be that as it may, the crates of fizzy drinks were set out in the kitchen at home as though we were preparing for a wedding and the visits of friends never let up. They came to me, or spoke to me on the phone, every day. They followed with me blow by blow the news relating to my studies. Some of them were people whom I hadn't thought had ever realized I'd been away.

One of my visitors during this period was Brother Jamal, 'the Living Martyr,' who had carried out the Jama'a's first suicide mission, dedicated to the assassination of Zaki Badr, the interior minister. The martyr was still alive because the explosive device in the pickup truck that lay in wait for the minister's cavalcade failed to detonate fully. This colleague of mine at medical school received partial burns and was arrested and tortured to a degree that went beyond anything the brothers had heard of or experienced, despite which he gave away no information whatsoever and the case against him collapsed and he was not brought to trial. We would go out and walk in the side streets and talk about everything concerning the brothers and Islamist action. He advised me to put my time in prison behind me and he told me that Sheikh Mahmud knew well that one of the senior brothers – the Brothers of '81 – had been chosen to take part in the attempt to overthrow the regime that took place immediately following the assassination of Sadat but had at the last moment withdrawn, and that the brothers understood and empathized with this decision. Jamal was unaware at the time that I had gone beyond that stage and arrived at a point where the problem was with me myself, with convincing my 'mathematical' mind to invest more in the side of the equation that related to sacrifice. I was no longer convinced. The equation, as I saw it, was chemical, not algebraic, and in such equations the elements differ in their essence and in their original nature, not just in their quantities. The first thing I learned after coming out of prison was to think in detail about subjects in an attempt to arrive at the correct names for actions and feelings and, more importantly, at the questions and answers that would give expression to oneself, with all one's strengths and weaknesses, with everything one loved and hated, with the whole spicy mix in which one's flesh and bones were steeped, and that gave one a particular taste. Taste, in particular, was a very relative matter. Lentil soup poured over rice was a tasteless and unappetizing dish, and lentil soup with no spices whatsoever poured over rice boiled in tap water was disgusting. Nevertheless, I had now come to love it. The stewed beans that the inmates of the upper-level cells loved to prepare had become my specialty. I would leave the oil on the fire while I cut up the tomatoes and peppers and then put them into it and take my time before mixing them together. Then I'd add the mixed spice and the beans and a clove of garlic. When I now tasted the first mouthful of this near daily meal, it was like swallowing memory pills "to be taken every night before bedtime." Prison – short though my stay there was – is a psychological experience that can be understood only by those who have lived through it. One part of it consists of fear of the person who owns the keys to the doors: he can at any moment start a fight with you and then shoot you; he can pour water into your cell, thus denying you sleep for days and nights on end, or isolate you some place where your tongue grows heavy for want of speech and the pupils of your eyes grow large from the constant darkness. It was the other part of it, though, that stayed with me when I could forget about the one with the keys. Survival between four walls touched a love of solitude in me. I spent my safe leisure hours at home inventing worlds, summoning up deeds and characters, and wresting these from their contexts and then putting them into new contexts and observing them. From this perspective, one could grow to love rather than hate the characters, or to empathize with them after rejecting them cruelly, or to mock them after having treated them with reverence, or to vent one's rancor on things one had tolerated. Large is the Lego set of the world inside the narrow cell, and vast the universe imprisoned inside the brain of man!

Mamduh visited me a number of times after I left prison. He had been my friend for four years. While preparing for Secondary General certificate we'd taken private lessons together in the same group, and we were colleagues at medical school. One evening he saw me in front of our house and said, in astonishment, "Your face is so full of light! It must be because you finished memorizing the Qur'an before you went into prison." His eyes remained trained on my face, as though he were witnessing the appearance of a holy vision. "Come off it. It's not full of light or anything," I said. I didn't want to laugh because Mamduh was excessively sensitive. "Take a good look," I continued. It seemed that each of us was being careful to avoid saying anything that might hurt the other's feelings but I took the initiative in offering an explanation. After two months without being exposed to the sun, my complexion had to be a little lighter and given that I had shaved off my black beard at noon that same day, the effect must have been heightened. In fact, my face was more like a lemon – yellow, and thin, with protruding bones. A few days after coming out of prison, I had started taking quite large doses of antibiotics to treat what was a chronic bronchitis, according to the doctor's diagnosis. The past two weeks hadn't been time enough for me to make up for the bad nutrition.

This was the second time I'd shaved off my beard. The first had been two years before, when the security situation in Asyut had deteriorated and I was in my first year of college. That day my uncle had stood next to me as I shaved it off, to make sure that I wouldn't go back on my word and lose my resolve at the last minute. The family was in shock because my father's sister's son had been arrested even though he wasn't a member of the Jama'a Islamiya in any way, shape, or form; his name had been found in the phone book of a colleague of his at the university who had been arrested a few days before. My family had no doubt that I would be arrested too. I shaved my face weeping, like one who sees his foot being cut off before his eyes. After that I hadn't laid a razor to it and had let it grow naturally, in the hope that by the time my beard had grown back, the crisis would have come to an end. On this second occasion, I showered, and stepped out of the shower without a beard. My father was in the house with me. He still had that same gaze that could see anything in the world but my face, as though it were transparent. When my mother came back from work, my sister apprised her in the kitchen of what I had done, saying in a whisper, "Mama, Khaled has shaved off his beard." My mother came out as if she had already had her share of surprises during my absence and there was no need as far as she was concerned to react to anything new about me.

I had no idea what would happen to my beard after that but I needed to use the opportunity to get a taste of freedom, to walk down the main street and not keep to the side streets, and to do so without fear of being watched or followed or arrested. I didn't want to attract people's attention, and so make them watch my behavior. Men with beards did not usually sit by the Nile and rest their heads on its iron balustrade or stroll along its banks, nor did they flick their key chains as they walked and then wind them round one finger before flicking them back again. They were even less likely to whistle, or hum under their breaths the tune of a popular song that was going through their minds. They didn't sit in cafés where informers were likely to be found playing backgammon and smoking a hookah. Just as standing out from the herd, with my beard and clothes, had once given me pleasure, now melting into their midst gave me a sense of limitless freedom, as though I'd discovered a cloak that made me invisible. I would pass my hand over where my beard had been and if after a few hours it met with the roughness of sprouting hairs, I'd go back to the bathroom and apply the razor to them. I thought that all well-dressed men did the same. My chin became inflamed and the place where my beard had started on my neck flushed with brown pimples, thus teaching me the basics of shaving – the direction of the hair, the nature of the skin, the appropriate toiletries. I was now invisible among ordinary people and conspicuous among the brothers when I went to the mosque. I therefore shifted to praying in a mosque where everyone else looked like me, where their faces were the same color as mine, or at least weren't differentiated from it by that conspicuous black border. My presence among them didn't add a great deal and they didn't notice my absence when I chose to pray at home on my own, in private communication with God, in a place where feet didn't touch other feet, or shoulders other shoulders – just private prayer, complaint, confession, and contemplation. Even reading, which I loved, didn't take the same large share of my time during this initial period. My main concern was to do well in my studies, and it called for extra effort to keep my morale high and my motivation alive, in view of the fact that I was not certain of winning the case that we had brought against the university to make them rescind my suspension. I did, however, read a play by Tawfiq el-Hakim that had a great effect on me. In it, the hero of the piece, poor but descended from kings, refuses to walk in the second row, directly behind the leader, and insists on walking in the rear, not out of modesty, but because the role of second man, lost in the middle of the throng and receiving direct orders, was not for him.

The Jama'a was absolutely right to insist on collective action. Individual action strips a person down to his eternal, infinitely ancient weakness, in one sense, and, in another, to his eternal, infinitely ancient strength, neither of which is conducive to group thinking. A person's weakness comes to the surface in the face of his senses and desires in a direct confrontation where no one else can help and which no one else can monitor. His or her strength, however, lies in discovering these desires and acquiring the right mixture of flexibility and firmness when dealing with them, in undergoing the anxiety of decision-making, and in attaining the deeper perspective created by diversity. More important still is his/her greatest strength, in the general human sense, which lies in the fact that every individual differs genetically, intellectually, psychologically, and socially from every other individual in the world. A simple but radical fact. It implies that every individual possesses the capacity to add qualitatively to a group rather than being just a unit in what the Qur'an calls *a building well-compacted* (61:4). It also implies that every individual is a sculpture, different in color and shape, rather than a stone indistinguishable from its peers in this mighty edifice that we call the world, or humankind. We are always being warned against self-conceit, at home, at school, and by celebrities on television. No one, however, warns us against crushing modesty – the helplessness that makes one prey to the flies and vultures of the universe, allowing those who are no better than you to exercise a self-awarded authority over you. These consider themselves more courageous than you because they fight better. Fine, but you think better than they do, you can do algorithms better than they can. You read with greater concentration and absorb more than they do. You understand sciences they do not. You write better than they do. You preach as well as they do and better too. It doesn't diminish Kasparov that Larry Holmes is physically braver than he is, even if we concede for the sake of argument that to fight is to be brave and pay no attention to the moral courage that has nothing to do with physical violence. I, Khaled, am not a number and I will never be a number, to be sacrificed as part of a group that does not consider me qualified to know the name of its amir.

The Jamaʿa and the religion of Islam were absolutely right, and I prayed that God might bring them victory, sooner or later. I, however, did not deserve to be a partner in that victory. My heart was still attached to this world and my ego still retained its desire to be me. My mathematical mind told me that a simple analysis of my primary elements – my personal traits – indicated conclusively that I was of no use to them. From my release in mid-November until the date set for the delivery of the judgment in my case against the university in April of the following year, I never stopped going over in my mind the following idea – that a person, be he fat or thin, who is sickened by anything of a spherical shape, is unfit for an administrative or technical role on a soccer team, even if he loves the look of the boots, with their protruding cleats that look like a nanny goat's nipples. Every attempt of this cleat-loving, ball-hating person to find a role for himself on the team will cost him an opportunity to discover in himself other capacities, such as coming up with a way to touch the udders of the goat and thus obtain a greater flow of milk. I had no talents apart from the ability to memorize and to write, both of which were of no value. The Jama'a needed people capable of jihadist action, for which I had neither capabilities nor talents. I would tell myself, "I will belong to the Islamist movement when it has a role for my talents, when the boxing match is over and the chess game begins, or even (and this was very important) when the boxing match and the chess game coincide."

The eve of the day when the court sentence was to be pronounced, I stayed up all night and didn't go to sleep before seven in the morning so as to avoid the anxiety of the last moments. I woke up, however, to the sound of loud heartbeats coming from my chest, even though my father still hadn't phoned to inform us of the result. Then he did so, and it became my duty to screw my zeal to the sticking point for the remaining two weeks before the exams. For the first time since I'd joined the Jama'a, I got exam nerves. I would remind myself of the promise I'd made myself when I was blindfolded and waiting for interrogation – that nothing after that day would scare me. All the same, I was anxious and the promise was now just a mirage. Failure now would be a disaster; everything would be lost, and I'd end up with neither this world today, nor the next world tomorrow.

✳

Six years had passed between my joining the university and the Barcelona Olympic Games. During this period, from 1986 to 1992, and even after my release from prison seven months earlier,

I hadn't sat down openly to watch television, with the exception of a religious or a political program (during which I would avert my face if a woman appeared as a guest) or sometimes to watch a soccer match. The Olympic contests are neither movies nor songs, with all that these two genres entail by way of entertainment and even, sometimes, lewdness. They are just sporting competitions. They do, however, have women who bare parts of their bodies that religion forbids us to see. All the same, there is a small difference that made the games the appropriate occasion for the chain of events that led to my public shift in attitude toward the television: the nakedness of the women is not accompanied by any lewdness that might lead to embarrassment or require of me a body language expressive of disgust, followed by my leaving the place entirely. The magic of the gymnastics and their harmoniousness when linked to rhythm, the slim bodies, cutting like swords, in the swimming competitions, and the strength and determination displayed in the pole vaulting take the mind far from thoughts of the competitor's body as a forbidden sexual object and stimulator of lust.

Or so it is with most people, though I will not fool myself that that is how I felt. That day, when I watched the half-dressed women on television for the first time as I lay stretched out, secure and not bothering to conceal myself, on the sofa in front of the television, with the rest of the family either sitting around me or coming and going, I focused on the crease beneath the roundness of the buttocks that appeared when a female gymnast, her curves clearly outlined, stretched her body in order to salute the spectators or when a female pole vaulter stood erect in the moments when she concentrated all her forces before the jump, and on the smooth cylinder of the thigh of a woman that was either wet, or about to become so.

Later, my sister told me that my mother had expressed her anxiety that I had seen women on the television while watching the Olympics, which was understandable at that time of major transformations, among which this behavior of mine might be counted. The shaving of one's beard was a momentous matter, but it had occurred before from time to time for security reasons or because of things that had to do with the position of a Jama'a member vis-à-vis his family. There were many brothers, especially those who lived with their families, who were obliged to shave their beards when they left prison. Not going regularly to the Jama'a's mosque might fall into the same category. These were all temporary changes, or so others believed, and so the committed individual would himself be convinced. Such a conviction leaves the rope by which one might one day climb back in one's hand, like the detached tail of a lizard. Watching scantily clad women on television, however, was an act that nobody had forced me to undertake, and it represented a breach in my perspective on what was allowed and what was forbidden. It wasn't possible to delay this or to hide it, as I had done in the past. I did quite well in 'the world's' exams. I expected that I would get a final grade of Good, which would allow me, legally speaking, to transfer my papers to Cairo University, and this is indeed what happened. I didn't want to do there, where no one would see me, what I wouldn't do here under their eyes.

I would pray the afternoon prayer in my sister's apartment, which had been left empty by her husband's departure for Saudi Arabia and her moving in with us in Asyut till his return. Four months had passed since my move to Cairo. I lived in a district where I knew no one and I had no friends at the university. The streets were filled with endless noise – from the wandering vendors who called their wares, from the vegetable sellers who had their vegetables spread out on the sidewalk from early morning until the afternoon, from the voices of the children who played in the street and the young men who stood around in groups joking loudly with one another, and from the mothers calling to their children to get washed or get on with their homework. The noise was too much for me if I opened a window and sat in front of it to study as I had used to do at home, but when I closed the double-glazed windows the noise was transformed into total silence. In summer, the heat was unbearable because there was no other apartment above mine. I didn't want to turn on the air conditioning because that would inflate the electricity bill that my sister had to pay on her 'empty' apartment and so as not to wear the appliance out before she and her family returned. In winter, the cold insinuated itself into my very bones. The carpets had been taken up before my sister moved to our house and the furniture covered, except for the bed that I used, two wooden chairs, and a movable table; these last I moved from place to place.

The phone rang while I was performing the second prostration of the prayer. There wasn't enough time to complete the remaining two prostrations before this rare sound would cease, and I couldn't interrupt my prayer, the link between the worshiper and his Lord. Believers of the righteous first generations of Muslims had been totally cut off from any awareness of what was around them when they entered the presence of the Merciful, to the degree that one of them who had been wounded in battle and had been obliged to have his foot cut off embarked on his prayer and completed it, unaware of the pain of the amputation, which had been per- formed without anesthetic. I had never known such a feeling and nor did I expect to feel it, since the man in question had gone down in history for doing so. At the least, though, I made an effort to be submissive in prayer, to think about what I was reading from the Qur'an, and to expel thoughts of this world from my heart while engaged in the five obligatory daily prayers.

Uttering the words "I seek the forgiveness of Almighty God," I broke off and ran toward the phone. All that was on the other end was a worker from the telephone company checking the lines in the area following complaints. I sat on the floor and wept, more than I had done in prison, though at least there was nobody with me here to judge my crying a sign of weakness.

Using personal contacts, we tried to ensure a room in the Uni- versity City student housing. That would save me the bother of having to think about food and drink, since the university pro- vided meals for the students there. It would also save the expense and inconvenience of transportation. It was a ten-minute walk from the university housing to my college, while my present accommodation was more than an hour and a quarter from there using public transport. Our contacts failed to bypass the rules preventing transfer students from residing in University City, especially in the first year after their transfer. It wasn't so much that these rules were observed as that my contacts were so weak that all I was able to succeed in doing was to reserve a room in my college for the period of its final exams, which came late, after the students at the other colleges had finished theirs and vacated their rooms. I finished the year with a grade of Very Good. Such a grade was no longer considered outstanding at medical school, but it wasn't too bad given my circumstances and was an encouragement at the end of a year of living away from home. Our cohort at the college was divided into groups on an alphabetical basis, with the exception of one group that brought together a small minority of students who had taken make-up exams the year before and a majority who were transfer students. This was the group I was in. We were strangers, living in our fourth academic year like first-year students, surrounded by others whose networks of friends had been in place for the past three years. Throughout the year, I'd got to know only a small number of people – though enough to be aware that a City Boy (a student living in University City) was someone from the countryside who put his spoon in his university bag and ran off fast at the end of classes so as to catch the university cafeteria before it closed. And, where relationships were concerned, City Boys were for City Girls. The pretty girls whom I saw on campus didn't take City Boys as boyfriends: "Do you want her friends to say she's going out with a City Boy?" Thank God, then, that I was not a City Boy.

There was a City Girl who wore a modest headscarf and was quiet whom I liked. However, I discovered that she loved a City Boy who, like her, was from Fayoum; a stolid, obnoxious youth who got Excellent each year. Like any hero in an Egyptian movie, I believed that obviously they couldn't be happy in their life together so long as I was thinking about her and she wasn't thinking about me. I switched her for another girl, who aroused the mirth of a Cairene friend. "How can anyone love a girl with a big pelvis and thin calves?" he said. I stopped loving her. I wanted to get to know the girls in the groups of friends who sat together in the lecture halls. One of the transferees in our group had got to know one of them and she had invited him to her birthday party. Should I try with that girl, who dyed her hair red? Or with that other one, who wore a shirt open at the neck that revealed the top of her breasts when she bent forward? Some of these girls were friends with a fellow student in my cohort who went around with a lollipop in his mouth. What should I do? I was still a cocoon, not a caterpillar, or a butterfly; or perhaps more accurately, I was an eagle metamorphosing into an ordinary bird. I was no longer Brother Khaled, who had memorized the whole Qur'an and was ever ready to raise the fighting banner of Islam, but neither did I possess the vocabulary of the new world in which I lived. Even if I became a bird, I'd never put a lollipop in my mouth. I saw an exhibition of Palestinian wounded put on by the Muslim Brotherhood at our college. My friend gave a contribution of one pound and I gave a contribution of twenty and kept repeating all the way back to my house that I was nothing, nothing, and that the twenty pounds, which meant a lot to me, meant nothing to God.

The only people I found with whom I could share anything throughout the entire year were the Ahli soccer club fans. At the Ahli club itself, where the membership fees were thousands of pounds, I would enter the team's training pitch via a special passage for the plebeian fans and there enjoy the company of those cheering for a team I loved, not least because it was recovering its strength after three years during which it had failed to regain the league trophy. I thought about forming a fan club based on a civilized, urban style of applause and encouragement that did not depend on insults that my clean tongue still couldn't bring itself to pronounce. Then I abandoned the idea and stopped going because the people who went there weren't like me either.

Finally I ran into some familiar faces. I saw the Living Martyr and another brother, who was also called Jamal, with whom I'd a reasonably good relationship because his sister had been a student in the same year as me at Asyut. I saw the two of them walking in a side street past a store selling sugar-cane juice on the road that goes between the Qasr el-Aini Hospital, where I was studying, and the Sayyida Zeinab metro station, where I would catch the underground train to go home. In an instant, this appallingly huge city, in which a man could insult another by calling his mother a whore and where the subsequent quarrel would come to an end without bloodshed and without the family being rent asunder because the mother of the person insulted was the wife of the maternal uncle of the son of the paternal uncle of the person who uttered the insult, was turned into a small town. One could count from one to ten and learn by heart the shapes of the numbers in between, or from one to a thousand, or even to ten thousand, but this face was one among fifteen million. The Living Martyr was my last pleasant memory of the Jama'a Islamiya; his was the one cheerful face in the midst of the darkness after I left the prison. The moment I reached him and called out his name, he would hug me, and perhaps kiss my hands; he certainly wouldn't let go of them as long as we were talking. The sight of him brought back a past that I'd left behind only a few months before but which now seemed far gone.

I went straight into the juice place and hid my face behind a tankard of white juice that was almost too sugary to drink, so that I had to ask the man to add some lime juice to it. I didn't emerge until the two brothers had disappeared from sight and then proceeded on the alert, measuring my steps so that I could hide behind a wall or a fruit barrow should I suddenly find them in front of me. The past wasn't far enough away for me yet; I was like one of a couple who have separated and who fears that the excitement of an encounter will make him forget the bitterness he has lived through. And I was again reassured that I was nothing. I was afraid; afraid and wanted to hide. During the summer vacation I didn't return to Asyut but remained in the emptiness of Cairo, with all its torpor.

At the beginning of my fifth year, the lawyer from the Legal Affairs department of Cairo University sent me a letter summoning me for interrogation and claiming that I had taken part in student agitation during the month that I had spent in University City. I knew they were preempting any request I might make to the university for accommodation there, which was now my right. They did not know that I no longer wanted to be a City Boy.

At the interrogation I thanked the university for hosting me for a month in student housing and said that these were slanders that I knew the university had to investigate; however, I undertook not to present a request for housing in University City as proof of my good intentions.

✳

When Esam, a new friend of mine from Cairo University, saw me playing soccer with my friends in the college, he said I was the person his five-a-side team needed, or so he told me a while later, when he reproached me for the deterioration of my standard. I play with my left foot as well as I do with my right, a skill I gained by imitating Eder, the Brazil left wing at the 1982 World Cup, and then from occupying the position of left midfielder when I started training regularly with Asyut's Welidat district team a year later. I never played soccer with a major team, as I had hoped, and I didn't even continue training with Welidat for more than two seasons. I was about five years younger than most of the players. With the exception of four or five, the players were all from the same poor quarter of Asyut. The more seasoned players didn't go to school and didn't like the "moma's and poppa's kids." With us on the team was a bandy-legged dwarf whose true age no one knew and who had a friend aged eighteen, who, were it not for his weak physique, could have been a star player on a major team. These two enticed a boy two years older than me (I was then twelve) into a deserted building and assaulted him sexually, then told everyone on the team, so that the boy became the object of everyone's mockery. Naturally, I felt afraid. At the same time, interest in the team, which was supposed to be Asyut's best, was low. We were no longer given a bag containing a complete sports uniform, and even the hot meal that was provided after training had been changed to one of dried meat, something that, in Egypt at least, is always of dubious quality.

Soccer, however, remained in my fate, disappearing and then reappearing. When I got to know Esam's team in the fifth year, I had become more at ease with my life in Cairo. Playing soccer and getting exercise were a part of it, but the companionship was more important. Through these players, who included the colleague with the lollipop, I made friends with people who held a literary salon where they would read what they had written. There I discovered the meaning of concision, and the difference between the image and the simile, and between poetry as meter and rhyme and poetic language as a means to express an idea. After college, Hasan and I would go for walks and he would read me verse about a seller of limes who sold five limes for a piaster, an image that I had never imagined could be appropriate for poetry. Hasan smoked, while I did not. He drank Turkish coffee, which I didn't. He told me that tobacco and coffee were the universal breakfast of intellectuals – a collective ritual that did not attract me. I prayed and he did not. He spoke to me about new movies; I watched movies for free on the television but wouldn't pay money to commit a sin such as entering a cinema. I didn't tell him this. I didn't tell any of my college friends that I was a member of the Jama'a Islamiya. Even when one of them made fun of fatwas issued by one of the four great imams, I would argue with him without being obstinate. Hasan's culture was entirely non-religious. He'd insult whoever he felt like among the big names in cinema, poetry, and the novel, finding fault with this one and that. I listened without comment because I had no idea what he was talking about. When he spoke of Islamic matters, however, I discovered he was ignorant about some of the things he talked about. I liked him because there were things he knew and things he didn't and he didn't behave as though he thought he was perfect. His right hand had only four and a half fingers, the little one being cut short. How had I not noticed that before? It was very obvious when he was holding a short story to which I'd made some changes. He told me that I was a quick learner, and that encouraged me. Hasan was two years older than me. Would it be possible for me, after two years, to know as much about literature as he did? On my next visit to my parents' house, I went down to the damp room in the basement of the building, where books lay scattered on the floor, the cardboard boxes in which we had put them for storage two years before having broken open. I took the novels of Naguib Mahfouz, the plays of Tawfiq el-Hakim, and the memoirs of Muhammad Hussein Heikal concerning life in Egypt before the Revolution.

Reading wasn't my sole pastime on that trip to Asyut. I had obtained the telephone numbers of two girls in our street. They couldn't believe that it was I who was speaking to them. They repeated their exclamations of astonishment again and again, but I paid no attention. I wanted to sleep with a woman. I was twenty-three years old and had never done so. I wanted to feel in Asyut what I couldn't in Cairo, that I was a man who was desired. Even more to the point, I could not resist that greatest of human temptations. By the time I returned to Cairo, I had become an addict of Indian films, sometimes watching three in a single day. I did it exclusively to watch the bodies of the women as they shook, and then when their clothes clung to their bodies in the obligatory scene under the rain, or when the man runs his eyes over the heroine's body till they reach her backside and he then turns his gaze to the camera like a doctor listening with his ear to the patient's body. Afterward I would go out and smoke a water pipe and watch the girls passing by in the street.

I gave up these habits when, via a soccer friend, I got to know a girl, one this time who didn't wear a headscarf and was extremely self-confident. I would think about her before I went to sleep and wake up in the darkness to see her face in detail like a moon inhabiting the room, in the highest corner furthest from my bed. I wrote a story about twins, one of whom was serious, the other reckless and irresponsible, and a girl who loved the reckless and irresponsible one even though he was not true in his love for her. The girl had the name of the girl I'd met and the good twin had mine. She didn't like it when she read it and she told me so with annoyance, giving me a look that implied I was stupid. It seems she'd understood! I'd go with their group of friends on every trip they went on. I committed to heart once more the songs of Abd el-Halim Hafez that I'd forgotten and insist on playing the same songs over the speaker system of the bus, the songs carrying by their nature the message of the faithful lover. I would return with dreamy romanticism to an agonizing moralism, obtuse and tired in its expressions. I was a sprout born without that certain something that makes the sunflower turn its face, the blossoms of the columbine close and open. I bought a BTM shirt and two day-glo jackets, one red, the other blue. Then I became embarrassed by them – two awful colors from a fashion I didn't understand. I sent one to my uncle on my father's side without even wearing it and carried the other over my arm, making do with a shirt in the December cold. I listened to foreign songs because she liked them and as though I was going to be examined on them at the end of the course. I tried everything that I thought might make me attractive in her eyes. By nature, though, women choose according to implacable criteria. Her friend informed me that her opinion of me was that "he thinks he's Abd el-Halim Hafez." I was too disturbed to withstand so much as a breath of disapproval and certainly not a bullet like that. On the other hand, I was in need of a puff of wind to make me fall from the thin thread on which I swung and to blow me hither and thither, no matter where it came from. I sat on the bed in my darkened room, imagining myself as a pair of socks rolled inside out and revealing what was within. I didn't know who I was. I played roles that were not meant for me. I inhabited the roles well and believed each time that this was I. What mendacity and what truth at one and the same time! I would watch myself and applaud. A hero for one hour, an anti-hero for the next. The viewer is confused: the actor is playing two roles with the same competence and the same feeling. And the actor is confused: the viewer applauds throughout the two hours. I didn't like college or the lectures any longer, and I couldn't concentrate on my lessons.

I bought a cinema ticket and went, for the first time in eight years. I remember the day well because it was the day when I excused myself from the exam in gynecology and obstetrics, the most important exam that year. I had promised my mother, after getting Very Good in the fourth year, that I would get Excellent in the fifth, and that day I realized that I would not be able to fulfill my promise. The movie I watched was called *Kashf al-mastur* (Revealing the Hidden), about a prostitute who works for a department of the secret police, gathering information on politicians' scandalous doings. After she repents of her life as a prostitute, the secret police blackmail her with the tapes she has made to force her to return to her profession; she has only to change roles, in keeping with the proverb (noted by an actress in the movie) that says, "When the prostitute retires, she turns pimp."

Beneath a broken street lamp we found the quiet, dark spot we'd been looking for with unspoken complicity. It was on the sidewalk that runs by the Nile, opposite the Hotel Semiramis. As we had walked from Garden City to the Corniche, we had talked of the common interest that our brief acquaintance had allowed us to find – the role of the narrator in documentary cinema. I had recently joined a course at the Cinema Palace and was on my way home from there. Like any enthusiastic novice, I wanted to show off what I knew and loved others to know my opinions. I was now closer to the age Hasan had been when I had got to know him about a year before. Every day I read, with greater or lesser attention, a hundred and fifty pages in the Mubarak Public Library that had opened close to my college at the beginning of that year, 1995. After that, I would go to the British Council to study English and borrow movies twice a week, and once a week to the Cinema Palace, to watch a European movie, and once more each week to study the general principles of cinema. I was trying to make up for the 'worldly' culture that I'd missed out on. I had more time now that, at the start of the sixth and final year of medical school, I'd decided that I would never practice medicine, though I would continue my education. I had started working as an intern at *al-Ahram al-riyadi* (al-Ahram Sports), on the basis that journalism was the closest profession to being a writer and a thinker – or something of that sort, I didn't know exactly what, which was my dream. After my six-year experience with the Jama'a, the next six years of my life during which I'd studied medicine had been a sacrifice, and not simply a little pocket change to be handed out in tips. There was no escaping my decision, though. I felt as if there was a bird in my chest that wanted to get out. Going out onto the balcony to take the air was not enough to drive away my feeling of claustrophobia, nor was crying enough to shed my melancholy. During that period, my sense of self grew to an exceptional degree, like a genie wanting to be released and to decide at least a meager part of its fate. I was reading Abd el-Rahman Badawi's translation of Sartre's work *L'Être et le néant* and Dr. Yaser, who had helped me to get the job with al-Ahram Sports, told me that I'd got to it too late, fifty years after it had been in fashion.

I helped her sit on the cement wall that followed the course of the Nile, and her feet didn't touch the ground. The fashion in Egypt at that time was dresses with buttons in front from top to bottom. When she sat down, bits of her thigh could be seen. I hesitated but I didn't want to waste any more time. I turned my back to the street so that I was facing her and, behind her, the Nile. I extended my fingers between two buttons and touched her thigh. She opened one button to facilitate the task. With my right hand I touched the underside of her right thigh. With her left thigh she pressed on my hand to keep it where it was. It wasn't the first time I'd put my hand on a woman. Some months before, at the cinema, I'd groped a girl whom I'd got to know over the telephone, but I knew she was 'easy,' so it didn't involve any great skill on my part. This was the first time I took a risk. Also recently I'd watched a movie with explicit sex and, for the first time in my life, seen a woman naked and seen a 'real' sex act. The experience this time, though, had a different feel to it. Her thigh wasn't completely smooth; it wasn't 'cream' or 'Turkish delight' but had small hairs that I could feel under my fingers. I wanted to go on all the same. This was a very good sign: it meant that the visceral disgust that had afflicted me after the movie and that was still with me was a temporary symptom. I didn't hate women in their real form, even if sex was no longer an act enframed by roses and women no longer hairless and light-filled creatures, but animals with anuses on whose bodies men deposited a mucus-like liquid. I don't think I wanted to sleep with her and I didn't want to go too far and attract attention. I was always nervous in any place where there were policemen: one of them might ask to see my I.D. or even take me in for investigation for any trivial reason and then discover who I was. Anyway, so far, it appeared, so good. The security guards at the hotel were far enough away to allow a degree of privacy and even a degree of safety: no passerby with suspicions about what we were up to would make himself obnoxious. There was nothing to worry about, unless by chance the presence of the security forces around this tourist location should lead us to talk of the Islamist groups and the state.

The previous year had witnessed qualitative shifts in Egypt. The police had killed Sheikh Tal'at Yasin, a prominent leader of the Jama'a, and a young man had attempted to assassinate Naguib Mahfouz. I didn't much like getting into detailed discussions of these events in case a slip of the tongue on my part should reveal my former relationship with the Jama'a. I had told a colleague at college that Naguib Mahfouz was a writer of genius but that from the Islamic point of view he was not a member of the religion, and my colleague had rejected my comment, asking, "What's that supposed to mean? That he's an unbeliever?" I didn't reply. In fact, I regretted having said what I had. It was difficult to explain my point of view without the extent of my knowledge of Islam attracting attention. Ironically, what I'd said concealed the reality of what I meant. The question of how one related to religion had become a major question mark in my life. The Caliph al-Mu'tasim, for example, was an unbeliever according to fundamentalist Islamists now and in the past because he believed that the Qur'an was created. However, when the Jama'a Islamiya wanted to attract young men to Islamic civilization they would say that al-Mu'tasim had dispatched armies to defend a single Muslim woman, captured by the Byzantines, who had cried "Alas, O Mu'tasim!" To me this now looked like pure opportunism and an admission on their part, to those who gave the matter a little thought, that the civilization of Islam did not only consist of the religion of Islam. 'Heretics' such as Ibn Rushd, Ibn Sina, and al-Ma'mun, and not just the religious scholars and the jurisprudents, were stockholders, perhaps majority stockholders, in Islamic civilization, just as Naguib Mahfouz, Taha Hussein, and, yes, even the Christian Salama Musa, were majority stockholders in today's Islamic civilization. What the religious scholars had to say about them would never hurt them, as long as the society was healthy and the scholars didn't claim more than was their due. That was what I'd meant. I was confused, though, didn't want to talk, and the victim of obsessive fears, of the authorities, and of the Jama'a, and the only solution was silence. It was the girl who spoke without reserve. She told me that her two brothers had been in detention for years, that she had worn a headscarf but later renounced it, and that she didn't know what would happen if either of her brothers were released. She wanted to change her life. She had read a novel by Edwar Kharrat and been much influenced by the character of the heroine. She recounted the plot to me in detail but I wasn't paying attention. Her brothers were in prison – a sentence to summon up all the ghosts from which I was in flight. I didn't lay another finger on her. I told her I was late for an appointment and thereafter avoided running into her until one day she asked me bitterly on the telephone, "What did I do?" I didn't answer. Perhaps her brothers had been with me in the prison to which the authorities had confined me, oppressed and incarcerated there without hope, and instead of protecting their 'honor,' I had been, on the contrary, aiding and abetting the tyrants against them.

I was the same person who had 'put a stop to the forbidden' with his air rifle nine years earlier. At the time I had believed that salvation lay there, and the strange thing was that I was still trying. When I was feeling disgusted, after watching the sex movie, I listened to a program on the radio hosted by a public figure at the time of the breaking of the fast during Ramadan. What caught my attention was that the guest was Dr. Muhammad Abu el-Ghar, my professor at medical school. He asked for a dish of beans, as he had become a vegetarian under the influence of the Hindu concept of the sublimity of the soul. As a result, I gave up eating the meat that I loved and became a vegetarian too. An aerial sprouted atop my head that was sensitive to every signal – a condition in which the universe conspires either to guide one rightly or to deceive one. Every word was an inspiration, every gesture a sign, especially when it came without warning. At a lecture on internal medicine, Dr. Husam Muwafi said that the Prophet (pbuh) had prayed to God to strengthen Islam through either Umar ibn al-Khattab or Amr ibn Hisham, even though they were both unbelievers at the time. "If people understood religion the way I do," he concluded, "they would realize that the Prophet evaluated people without regard for their religious affiliations." A wonderful sentence. Thinking within a restricted space, as though in a tunnel, is a problem, and when one adds to that the claim that one knows what awaits people at the end of the tunnel, the problem is even greater. Why was Mustafa Mahmud's book *Rihlati min al-shakk ila-l-iman* (My Journey from Doubt to Faith) allowed to be published when Isma'il Ahmad Adham's *Limadha ana mulhid* (Why I Am an Atheist) was not? They both started off together but the first arrived at the inevitably approved conclusion, whereas the second did not. The reason is that there are people who don't think the way Dr. Husam Muwafi does, because there are societies that criminalize 'impeding the flow of traffic' but not 'impeding the flow of life' or 'impeding the flow of thought.'

Jean-Jacques Rousseau's *Confessions* is a wonderful book. He feels no shame about telling people that he did 'bad' things. In the end, this only makes him more human and constitutes a plea for tolerance. It opened up for me a golden road to something called 'autobiography,' the genre that provides examples of human experience of both debilitating pain and exhilarating joy, both reduced to fit between the covers of a book. The covers widen before me as I recall from my personal experience the tricks and games with time that reading can play. Killing pain is reduced to moving the concerned reader or causing the particularly sensitive reader to shed a couple of tears, and debilitating struggle and devastating anxiety to a frisson or a widening of the pupils. What a price for the reader to pay!

Babette's Feast is a wonderful movie, though most of the audience at the Cinema Club couldn't sit through it to the end. The French-born serving girl inherits a huge fortune. She goes to Paris and returns to the puritanical Danish household where she works and prepares for them all sorts of delicious dishes. The camera pans poetically over the different types of food as they are being prepared, then over the faces as they savor them. They eat and drink wine, and then they talk, staying up late and dancing. The puritanism disappears, to be replaced by tolerance. Then the camera focuses on the expressions of astonishment on the faces of her employers when they realize that their maid has spent her entire fortune on this feast. Are a few moments of humanity worth such a price?

Arthur Miller's *The Crucible* made me weep like a madman, and damn and curse, and curse, and curse. Next I read *On Liberty* by John Stuart Mill and it was as though I had reached the Promised Land and had the right, finally, to throw my cross off my shoulders – no absolute authority of any sort; no one to decide what I should read or listen to; no one to impose on me their paradigm, their own interpretation of history, or their own aspirations for the future; no one to take me to task when I had committed no wrongdoing, while they did wrong without being held to account.

> Until today my friend I would deny,
> If his beliefs with mine did not concur.
> Now my heart is open to all kinds,
> Is a monastery for monks, a meadow for the deer,
> A house for idols and a Ka'ba for the pilgrim's round,
> A codex for the Qur'an and tablets for Moses's law,
> For Love my religion and my faith are now.
> Its creed it is that I profess, no matter where its mounts may veer.

Call Muhyi al-Din ibn Arabi an unbeliever if you wish. Call him a watermelon if you wish. Just don't slice him in half with a knife, just as no one sliced al-Farabi or Ibn Sina, or Abu al-Ala' al-Ma'arri.

I am grateful to all of the above, as I am to that girl who took off her clothes in front of the camera and wiped the mucus-like fluid off her thighs, and, along with it, the scales from the eyes of a young man raised on illusions.

Glossary

Abd el-Halim Hafez One of Egypt's best-loved male singers. Born 21 June 1929, died of bilharzia 30 March 1977.

Abdel Nasser Gamal Abdel Nasser (1918–70): leader of the Free Officers movement that led to the overthrow of the monarchy in 1952, he served as president of Egypt from 1954 until his death.

Abu Hamid al-Ghazali Perhaps the greatest scholar of medieval Islam, al-Ghazali (1058–11) celebrated an approach to Islam that reconciled the shari'a with 'moderate' Sufism.

amir In the terminology of the Jama'a Islamiya, a team or group leader; literally, 'commander' or 'prince.'

Antar el-Absi Black pre-Islamic poet and hero of folk epic; lived during the second half of the sixth century AD.

Anwar Sadat President of Egypt from 1970 until his assassination in 1981 by members of the Jama'a Islamiya.

Camp David Accords Agreements reached in September 1978 between Egypt and Israel that led to the Egyptian–Israeli Peace Treaty in March 1979. Egyptians often refer to both as 'Camp David.'

Great Islamic Schism (*al-fitna al-islamiya al-kubra*) The struggle (657–61) between Ali ibn Abi Talib, fourth caliph of Islam, and Mu'awiya ibn Abi Sufyan, governor of Syria, for control of the Islamic empire. Partisans of the former and his descendants came to be known as Shi'a, those who accepted Mu'awiya's victory as Sunnis.

Hadith A 'tradition' or account of the words or deeds of the Prophet Muhammad. Hadiths supplement the ordinances found in the Qur'an and provide a model for the attitudes and comportment of the believer.

Hadith Qudsi A 'divine tradition,' consisting of an account of God's words revealed to the Prophet Muhammad but not included in the Qur'an.

hakimiya 'God's right to govern' a central concept of Islamist thought, used to counter the concept of 'the right of the people to govern.'

Ibn Arabi The greatest exponent of metaphysical Sufism (1165–1240).

Ibn Kathir Isma'il ibn Kathir (c.1300–73): expert on Hadith and historian of Damascus, who wrote a well-known commentary on the Qur'an.

Ibn Taymiya Ahmad ibn Abd al-Halim ibn Taymiya (1263–1368): conservative and literalist theologian whose denunciation of what he saw as heretical innovation in religious matters led to intense controversy. His views are today admired by 'fundamentalist' Islamic groups such as the Jama'a Islamiya and the Wahhabis of Saudi Arabia.

Ignorance Arabic: *Jahiliya*. Originally, the 'Days of Ignorance' before the rise of Islam; now also applied by Islamists to more recent times, in which Muslims have supposedly relapsed.

Imam al-Shafi'i Founder of one of the four canonical 'schools' of Islamic jurisprudence (767–820).

Imbaba A district of Giza (Cairo west of the Nile).

Isma'il Ahmad Adham Isma'il Ahmad Adham (1911–40): Egyptian writer and one of the few Muslim intellectuals to openly proclaim himself an atheist and defend his beliefs in writing.

Jama'a Islamiya One of the largest and most influential Islamist groups in Egypt. Its origins are a matter of debate, the Muslim Brotherhood claiming that the Jama'a began as its university arm, while the group itself claims to have arisen independently. The Jama'a Islamiya originally advocated a combination of covert armed action against the state with overt proselytization. In 1997, the group's imprisoned leadership called for the renunciation of violence.

Jam'iya Shar'iya A registered association that provides religious services (for example, running of mosques, information on the direction of Mecca from numerous locations, discussion forums) as well as relief and development assistance to Muslims in Egypt. Its largest mosque in Asyut functioned as the Jama'a Islamiya's main mosque until security forces took control of it in 1989.

jihad Arabic: 'struggle,' whether in the form of armed action for the expansion or defense of Islam (the 'physical' or 'lesser' jihad) or the Muslim's effort toward moral and religious perfection (the 'spiritual' or 'greater' jihad).

jihadist A political term used to describe an individual who believes that jihad is the most potent means to establish the rule of God on earth. The term was introduced into modern Islamic thought by the Egyptian Islamist writer, Abd el-Salam Faraj, who argued that the "absence of jihad" was the main reason for the weakness and retardation of the Islamic Nation.

Karam Zuhdi Member of the Jama'a Islamiya's Consultative Council, Zuhdi (born 1952) was imprisoned in 1981 following the assassination of Anwar Sadat and released in 2003.

Lazoghli A district of Cairo in which a number of government agencies are located, including the Ministry of the Interior and National Security headquarters.

Minya Provincial capital and province in Upper Egypt.

Muhammad Hussein Heikal Egyptian writer and politician (1888–1956). His novel *Zaynab* (1913) – which some critics see as the first true Egyptian example of the genre – describes the lives of peasants and advocates the rights of women.

Muhammad Qutb Islamist writer and activist (born 1919), brother of Sayyid; one of his persistent themes is resistance to western cultural as well as political hegemony.

Muslim Brotherhood A political movement founded in Egypt in 1928. Banned following its attempted assassination of Nasser in 1954, it was allowed to resume limited activity under Anwar Sadat but remains, formally speaking, an illegal organization.

al-Mu'tasim Caliph of the Abbasid dynasty; ruled 833–42.

Naguib Mahfouz Pioneering and prolific Egyptian novelist (1911–2006), awarded the Nobel prize for literature in 1988. In 1994, an attempt was made on his life following a death threat by a Jama'a Islamiya leader occasioned by the supposedly

blasphemous nature of one of Mahfouz's works and his
defense of Salman Rushdie.

Rabso An Egyptian detergent.

Ref'at el-Mahjub Speaker of the Egyptian People's Assembly,
assassinated in Cairo by members of the Jama'a Islamiya
in 1990. His killers were captured and confessed but their
convictions were later overturned on the grounds that the
confessions had been obtained under torture.

rub' Arabic: 'quarter.' The Qur'an is divided into 30 parts (*juz's*);
each *juz'* is divided into two *hizb*s; each *hizb* is divided into
four *rub's*.

Salafist Pertaining to the *salafi* Islamist movement, which
started in the nineteenth century in Egypt, and was committed
to gradualist reform.

Salama Musa Christian Egyptian writer and intellectual who
advocated Fabian socialism (1887–1958).

Satan had stopped urinating in his ear According to a Hadith,
"It was stated in the presence of the Prophet that a man slept
the night through until the morning and did not rise for the
[dawn] prayer. He said, 'Satan had urinated in his ear.'"

Sayyid Qutb Cardinal Islamist writer and activist (1906–66).
After making his mark as a literary critic (he introduced
Naguib Mahfouz to Egyptian readers), he joined the Muslim
Brotherhood in 1950 but became increasingly radical and
was the first to assert, in his *Ma'alim fi-l-tariq* (Landmarks
on the Road), that most Muslims are living in Ignorance (see
above). He was executed in 1966 but his works have provided
inspiration for many subsequent Islamist groups.

seven deadly sins In Islam, the seven deadly sins are
(according to a Hadith) "Polytheism, magic, taking a life
declared sacrosanct by God unless with due cause, usury,
embezzlement of the assets of orphans, flight in the face of
the enemy, and the defamation of women of unblemished
reputation." From these derive a number of major offenses,
such as theft, adultery, and the drinking of alcohol.

Shakespeare The words attributed to Shakespeare represent the author's memory of an Arabic translation of the passage from Hamlet, Act III, Scene 4 in which Hamlet asks:
"O shame! where is thy blush? Rebellious hell,
If thou canst mutine in a matron's bones,
To flaming youth let virtue be as wax,
And melt in her own fire: proclaim no shame
When the compulsive ardour gives the charge,
Since frost itself as actively doth burn
And reason panders will."

shari'a Literally, 'the path,' and hence the religious law of God, consisting of His ordinances as revealed in the Qur'an plus other acts of piety or obedience to Him.

Sheikh Umar Abd el-Rahman Born in 1938, Umar Abd el-Rahman emerged as a leader of the Jama'a Islamiya in the 1980s. Expelled from Egypt, he went to Afghanistan and later the United States, where he was convicted in 1995 of plotting acts of violence against U.S. civilian targets; he remains in prison in the U.S. In December 1998, he issued a statement from prison calling on Islamist groups to use only peaceful methods in their work.

Taha Hussein Writer, critic, and educator (1889–1973), and a major figure in the movement to introduce western canons of criticism into Egyptian scholarship.

Tal'at Yasin A leading member of the Jama'a Islamiya, Tal'at Yasin was arrested at the age of eighteen in the wake of their assassination of President Anwar Sadat in 1981. While in prison, he played a role in the reorganization of the Jama'a. Following his release three years later, he eventually rose, in the early 1990s, to become head of its armed, underground wing, which he led until killed by Egyptian police in 1994.

Umar ibn al-Khattab Second Muslim caliph (633–44), celebrated for his piety and wisdom.